Editor-in-Chief

NEW DIRECTIONS FOR YOUTH DEVELOPMENT

Theory
Practice
Research

spring | 2007

Transition or Eviction
Youth Exiting Care for Independent Living

Varda R. Mann-Feder — *issue editor*

JOSSEY-BASS™
An Imprint of
WILEY

Transition or Eviction: Youth Exiting Care for Independent Living
Varda R. Mann-Feder (ed.)
New Directions for Youth Development, No. 113, Spring 2007
Gil G. Noam, Editor-in-Chief

Copyright © 2007 Wiley Periodicals, Inc., A Wiley Company. All rights reserved. No part of this publication may be reproduced in any form or by any means, except as permitted under sections 107 and 108 of the 1976 United States Copyright Act, without either the prior written permission of the publisher or authorization through the Copyright Clearance Center, 222 Rosewood Drive, Danvers, MA 01923; (978) 750-8400; fax (978) 646-8600. The copyright notice appearing at the bottom of the first page of an article in this journal indicates the copyright holder's consent that copies may be made for personal or internal use, or for personal or internal use of specific clients, on the condition that the copier pay for copying beyond that permitted by law. This consent does not extend to other kinds of copying, such as copying for general distribution, for advertising or promotional purposes, for creating collective works, or for resale. Such permission requests and other permission inquiries should be addressed to the Permissions Department, c/o John Wiley & Sons, Inc., 111 River Street, Hoboken, NJ 07030; (201) 748-6011, fax (201) 748-6008, www.wiley.com/go/permissions.

Microfilm copies of issues and articles are available in 16mm and 35mm, as well as microfiche in 105mm, through University Microfilms Inc., 300 North Zeeb Road, Ann Arbor, Michigan 48106-1346.

NEW DIRECTIONS FOR YOUTH DEVELOPMENT (ISSN 1533-8916, electronic ISSN 1537-5781) is part of The Jossey-Bass Psychology Series and is published quarterly by Wiley Subscription Services, Inc., A Wiley Company, at Jossey-Bass, 989 Market Street, San Francisco, California 94103-1741. POSTMASTER: Send address changes to New Directions for Youth Development, Jossey-Bass, 989 Market Street, San Francisco, California 94103-1741.

SUBSCRIPTIONS cost $80.00 for individuals and $195.00 for institutions, agencies, and libraries. Prices subject to change. Refer to the order form at the back of this issue.

EDITORIAL CORRESPONDENCE should be sent to the Editor-in-Chief, Dr. Gil G. Noam, McLean Hospital, 115 Mill Street, Belmont, MA 02478.

Cover photograph by Lukasz Laska

www.josseybass.com

Wiley Bicentennial Logo: Richard J. Pacifico

Gil G. Noam, Editor-in-Chief
Harvard University and McLean Hospital

Editorial Board

K. Anthony Appiah
Princeton University
Princeton, N.J.

Peter Benson
Search Institute
Minneapolis, Minn.

Dale A. Blyth
University of Minnesota
Minneapolis, Minn.

Dante Cicchetti
University of Minnesota
Minneapolis, Minn.

William Damon
Stanford University
Palo Alto, Calif.

Goéry Delacôte
At-Bristol Science Museum
Bristol, England

Felton Earls
Harvard Medical School
Boston, Mass.

Jacquelynne S. Eccles
University of Michigan
Ann Arbor, Mich.

Wolfgang Edelstein
Max Planck Institute for Human Development
Berlin, Germany

Kurt Fischer
Harvard Graduate School of Education
Cambridge, Mass.

Carol Gilligan
New York University Law School
New York, N.Y.

Robert Granger
W. T. Grant Foundation
New York, N.Y.

Reed Larson
University of Illinois at Urbana-Champaign
Urbana-Champaign, Ill.

Richard Lerner
Tufts University
Medford, Mass.

Milbrey W. McLaughlin
Stanford University
Stanford, Calif.

Pedro Noguera
New York University
New York, N.Y.

Fritz Oser
University of Fribourg
Fribourg, Switzerland

Karen Pittman
The Forum for Youth Investment
Washington, D.C.

Jane Quinn
The Children's Aid Society
New York, N.Y.

Jean Rhodes
University of Massachusetts, Boston
Boston, Mass.

Rainer Silbereisen
University of Jena
Jena, Germany

Elizabeth Stage
University of California at Berkeley
Berkeley, Calif.

Hans Steiner
Stanford Medical School
Stanford, Calif.

Carola Suárez-Orozco
New York University
New York, N.Y.

Marcelo Suárez-Orozco
New York University
New York, N.Y.

Erin Cooney, Editorial Manager
McLean Hospital

Contents

Issue Editor's Notes *1*
  Varda R. Mann-Feder

Executive Summary *9*

1. Youth leaving care: How do they fare? *15*
   Anne Tweddle
   This chapter provides an overview of recent international research examining outcomes for youth after they age out of the child welfare system. It outlines recommendations for changes to practices and policies in facilitating the transition to independence.

2. The transition from state care to adulthood: International examples of best practices *33*
   Carrie Reid
   In order for youth to be prepared for the transition to adulthood, they must have key areas of their lives addressed: relationships, education, housing, life skills, identity, youth engagement, emotional healing, and adequate financial support. Successful and innovative programs for transition-aged youth in the United States, United Kingdom, and Australia are highlighted.

3. The role of housing in the transition process of youth and young adults: A twenty-year perspective *51*
   Mark J. Kroner
   Lighthouse Youth Services is a large housing-based independent living preparation program that has served over thirteen hundred youth and their children since 1986. This chapter describes housing options and basic program strategies, common problems, funding issues, and general outcomes for youth. The system characteristics necessary to make a program work are outlined, as well as key lessons learned.

4. Transition without status: The experience of youth leaving care without Canadian citizenship *77*
   Francis G. Hare
   Youth in transition from care sometimes lack legal status or citizenship. This may occur when a child arrived from another country alone or arrived with a family but was taken into care before status issues were resolved. The chapter examines the dimensions of this issue and the ways in which youth, service providers, and others have been working to minimize the numbers of young people who leave care without citizenship status.

5. Promoting autonomous functioning among youth in care: A program evaluation   *89*
Martin Goyette

This chapter describes a provincially funded program in Quebec that incorporates elements unique in the local child welfare system and preliminary findings on its impact. The program targets youth sixteen years of age and older who have had little family support, have exhibited high-risk behaviors, and are in the transition to independent living.

6. Juvenile offenders and independent living: An Irish perspective on program development with St. Xavier's   *107*
Niall McElwee, Michael O'Connor, Susan McKenna

The chapter views a specific population within the Irish social care system and draws from the authors' collective experience in relation to young offenders' leaving care. Effective program development for youth leaving care for independent living is considered crucial to potential long-term success and permeates all good practice.

7. The Scottish perspective: A pathway to progress?   *119*
Jeremy Millar

This chapter offers insight into the impact of reforms in terms of both direct work with care leavers in the northeast of Scotland and the broader aspirations of the new legislative framework. The author describes how the historical context that links Scotland to the Commonwealth (in terms of former approaches to practice and societal and demographic changes) have influenced practice and policymaking in this area.

8. Using youth expertise at all levels: The essential resource for effective child welfare practice   *139*
Kathi M. Crowe

Engaging youth as resources in all levels of child welfare work not only represents best practice, it is an essential ingredient to effective work. This chapter explores the benefits of drawing on youth expertise at both the micro and macro levels. The respect inherent in this inclusion assists the development of a stronger bond between staff and youth and results in more effective policies, programs, and services. The specific impact on the transition to independent living is discussed.

Afterword: Aging out of care—Toward realizing the possibilities of emerging adulthood   *151*
Jeffrey Jensen Arnett

INDEX   *163*

Issue Editor's Notes

TECHNOLOGICAL AND MEDICAL advances have done little to decrease the number of children at risk in the developing world. Instead, with the increased sophistication of reporting systems, there seem to be increasing numbers of children and adolescents whose development is seen as compromised, whether because of overt abuse, neglect, or an insidious pattern of parenting failures. Ultimately a significant proportion of these young people require removal from their homes.

Throughout recorded history, there has been a need to provide substitute care for children of all ages. The delivery of this care has changed radically over time, largely due to advances in our understanding of child development and the impact of parent-child attachment. At the beginning of the twentieth century, orphanages and large group settings were the placement of choice for even the youngest children. Over time, there has been a dramatic shift to smaller, more intimate settings, with a strong preference for substitute families wherever possible. At the same time, there is almost universal recognition that different children, depending on their history and the degree to which they have missed out on positive experiences, require different levels of structure and treatment. For this reason, being "in care" can refer to range of options along a continuum, ranging from the most normative and individualized at one end (adoptive family) to foster care, group home care, or residential placement at the other extreme. Children can have long-term placement in any of these options or move along the continuum through the course of a placement career. They can also be moved out of the system because they have attained the age of majority and can face the transition to independent living from the full range of placement resources.

Entering care

Parallel to the evolution of knowledge in child development and the creation of a range of care options, the universal rights of children for protection and care were embraced. The result has been that most countries now have legislation that necessitates intervention in families where children are in jeopardy. This means that the provision of substitute care has been judiciarized and that access to care, in most places where it exists, has been integrated into child welfare systems that include youth protection agencies, assessment services, and youth courts. Access to care is also linked in many places to juvenile justice legislation, where a period in placement may be viewed as a sentence. Criminal behavior on the part of children and adolescents can also expose their need for protection and substitute care. While the development of laws that protect children reflects efforts to improve lives, in practice they have resulted in a maze of bureaucratic structures that make entry into care a confusing and difficult process. This only serves to complicate an action, which by its very nature imposes a deeply wounding experience on a young person: removal from his or her family. In many instances, whether the child returns home or not, it takes a lifetime to work through the impact of entering care and the experience of placement.

Whether a child's removal from home takes place after long months of meetings and discussions or occurs abruptly in the context of a crisis, entering care is always a wrenching experience. It occurs in the context of failed relationships with significant others and imposes an overwhelming loss on a child, no matter at what stage it occurs. It is among the greatest personal tragedies that any child can face, even if it is invoked as a measure to relieve suffering and protect the child's future. Placement stimulates an emotional crisis, which can be characterized by rage, a deep sense of personal failure, helplessness, and sadness. Most young people who are placed have little voice in the matter; they are presented with ambiguous reasons for their removal from home and have little or no preparation. They face an unexplained and unpredictable future in unfamiliar surroundings, with only strangers to turn to for support. Individual differences among children entering care (age, attachment status, cognitive capacity, potential for emotional regulation) result in differential capacity to survive what can be understood only as massive trauma. And yet placement is still a necessary alternative for increasing numbers of children for whom remaining in their family of origin will result in repeated exposure to continuing abuse and neglect.

Being in care

A young person's ability to cope with the upheaval of placement and benefit from the care experience depends on many complex factors. Two central prognostic indicators are the availability of an appropriate placement resource and the child's capacity to work through his or her losses. It turns out that these two factors are in fact interrelated. In the presence of developmentally appropriate relationships and helpful treatment experiences, children can mourn, which allows them to move forward in their development. This is especially possible when care can be provided in a family setting, where appropriate parenting is available and the child can eventually make new attachments.

Although there are sometimes systemic barriers to placement in a family, there are often major problems among children coming into care that make placement in a family nearly impossible. Some youth coming into care are already so compromised that their chronic behavioral difficulties would exceed the coping ability of any family. In addition, children for whom the experience of removal from home is too overwhelming are often caught up in traumatic reenactments with adults that compel them to relive the original rejection or abandonment. In these situations, potential adoptive or foster home parents may lack the training or support needed to respond to the extreme challenges these young people present. Children in this latter situation are often placed directly in group care with the hope that they can make use of a less personalized setting in the transition back into a family. It is the most deeply damaged young people who spend their entire care career with no family.

Being in care is a highly individual experience. The circumstances of entry into care condition the experience of care because it may determine the placement setting, which is powerful in influencing the child's response and capacity to work through the transition. In addition, the range of placement options varies widely both within and between regions of the world. These discrepancies reflect differences in legal systems, the financing of services for children, and local values in relation to family preservation and youth protection. In real terms, this means that a child's placement history can be influenced by many factors above and beyond his or her individual needs.

The complexities of being in care present serious challenges to researchers. Nonetheless, outcome studies have proliferated, generally painting a mixed picture of the developmental status of youth who have been in care. It is generally accepted that children who have been in care can grow into healthy and successful adults; however, it has also been demonstrated that a significant proportion of care leavers will exit almost as emotionally and developmentally challenged as they entered. In these cases, the care experience may have at best forestalled and protected them from further injury in a compromised environment. At worst, it may have compounded preexisting difficulties to the point where the young person has becoming increasingly despairing and angry and faces the transition to adulthood without a sense of security, an education, or a meaningful support system.

Leaving care

There are as many possible trajectories out of care as there are pathways into it. Under optimal conditions, a placement is short and accompanied by intensive intervention that results in successful reinsertion into the natural family. Such cases require that parents and children are amenable to some form of treatment, that such treatment is available, and that the original conditions that led to placement are somewhat reversible. In the vast majority of cases, such an optimistic outcome is not realistic. The child may be ready to return to the family, but the family may be unable to receive the child. If there is extended family, this is the next best alternative. A third possibility is that the young person remains in care for so long, and with so little family support of any kind, that he or she must leave care to live independently. This discharge plan is usually the result of the young person's advancing age and the unfortunate reality that he or she may no longer be eligible to remain in the care system. Not only are these young people aging out regardless of their maturity level or readiness, they are compelled to function independently at a much earlier age than their peers who are not in care. Ironically, they have been much more compromised and yet have to grow up faster. Even among the population of youth leaving care, the group exiting for independent living has had the least support and may have the greatest challenges yet to face. The need to make the transition to independence magnifies gaps in a young person's background, as it calls for skill sets that are particularly unlikely to develop in long-term placement: autonomous behavior, self-care skills, and the capacity for self-soothing. At the best of times, launching into adulthood is an ambivalent process, which can stimulate self-doubt and a longing to be cared for. The ideal process among young adults leaving their family home is gradual and progressive and allows repeated attempts at leaving, returning, and leaving again. Not only are young people in care making the transition to independence without the benefit of positive attachments, they have no safety net or opportunity for repeated attempts at leaving. Compounding this is the reality that a transition out of care to a home of one's own confirms once again that a young person has lost his or her family.

To compound matters, leaving care restimulates unresolved issues related to placement. A young person leaving care to live independently must face that he or she has to become self-reliant and that the family of origin has never come through for him or her. This has been referred to in the literature as the need to remourn. This painful process can lead to regressive behavior just at the time when demands are being made on a young person to grow up. As they confront their losses once again, they may become enraged and noncompliant, or depressed and apathetic, resisting structure in a way that was characteristic of their functioning when they first came into care. Sometimes these youth cannot engage constructively in preparatory programs because they are so caught up in their feelings that they resist the transition out of care. Agencies and foster homes are not always able to tolerate this regression, and sometimes the result, ironically, is an abrupt discharge from care. It is for this reason that working with youth in transition to independent living is particularly challenging, and the creation of appropriate services is increasingly a concern for all who work with youth in care.

Conclusion

Placement in care is a response to the extreme circumstances of children and youth whose parents are unable to provide for their needs. It represents the best-intentioned efforts of child welfare and juvenile justice authorities to remove children from the most damaging home environments. It is the young people who are most deprived to begin with who actually remain in care long enough to age out, and they have no alternative but to attempt to move out on their own. It is not a matter of choice for them, and their readiness ultimately is not a determining factor. It is age alone that determines that these young people are no longer eligible for services. In this way, the transition from care to independent living can in fact be seen as an eviction.

The people and programs that work to facilitate the transition from care to independent living have a demanding mandate in relation to the continuum of services for youth. Not only are they charged with launching these young people into adult life against all odds, they are confronted with the unresolved wounds of each care leaver's accumulated experiences of loss, which culminates with the withdrawal of care at age of majority. In the course of confronting these losses, new behavioral and emotional expressions emerge that complicate the transition and try the resources of all involved. However, at the same time, intervening with these youth as they move out of care is a critical mandate. It offers a unique opportunity to launch a significant population of young people into independence while helping them to work through issues that represent significant obstacles to healthy functioning in adulthood. In many cases, it is possibly the only opportunity to help these young people move forward with optimism as they approach adulthood. It represents the last chance for agencies and service providers to fulfill their responsibilities to the children and young adults who have grown up in care.

This volume presents an overview of the issues that service providers, agency managers, and policymakers face in relation to the work with youth who are in transition to independent living from care. We begin with an excellent summary of the current state of knowledge about outcomes from Anne Tweddle. In Chapter Two, Carrie Reid then provides an outline of best practices from the United States, Canada, and Australia. Mark Kroner in Chapter Three offers an instructive overview of challenges and strategies in planning for appropriate housing for youth leaving care. In Chapter Four, Francis G. Hare presents the experiences of young people who make the transition to adult living without the benefit of citizenship or legal status. Chapters Five, Six, and Seven, by, respectively, Martin Goyette; Niall McElwee, Michael O'Connor, and Susan McKenna; and Jeremy Millar, present approaches to working with youth in transition from Quebec, Ireland, and Scotland. In the last chapter, Kathi M. Crowe highlights how youth engagement and empowerment can result in more meaningful practices and policies.

The chapters in this volume offer critical ingredients for transitional programs that can inspire hope for vulnerable young people and the professionals who work with them, thereby facilitating a transition rather than an eviction. The afterword by Jeffrey Arnett reviews these contributions and provides a critical link to developmental psychology, reaffirming that all of our efforts to support youth and young adults in care should be guided by an understanding of normative development.

Varda R. Mann-Feder
Editor

VARDA R. MANN-FEDER *is associate professor and chair of the Department of Applied Human Sciences at Concordia University in Montreal.*

Executive Summary

Chapter One: Youth leaving care: How do they fare?
Anne Tweddle

This chapter summarizes recent Canadian and international research on the outcomes for youth after they age out of the child welfare system. It paints a disturbing picture for this small and vulnerable population. Youth leaving care face many challenges in making the transition from state care to independence and adulthood. They bear the emotional scars of childhood neglect or abuse. They do not have a family support network, have limited or no financial resources, are often lacking in life skills, and usually have not completed school. Despite these setbacks, we expect them to function independently once they reach age eighteen.

Research shows that once youth leave care, they do not fare as well as their peers. They are at much greater risk of relying on social assistance, becoming homeless, engaging in substance abuse, becoming single parents, experiencing mental health problems, or coming into contact with the criminal justice system. Some youth aging out, however, have more successful transitions. These typically have completed high school, have role models, have access to postsecondary opportunities, refrain from alcohol or drug use, and obtain life skills and independent living training. Having stable placements while in care is also critical in ensuring more positive outcomes.

Canada does not have the capacity to track the outcomes of youth as they leave the child welfare system, nor can it identify

the types of interventions showing the most promise in helping them achieve better outcomes. Canadian governments need to improve their transitional planning for youth in care who are approaching the age of majority. Some recommendations include extending the age for services and financial assistance to age twenty-four, developing standards to prepare youth for leaving care, and exploring ways to enable youth to pursue higher education or training. Finally, Canada should develop a national longitudinal survey to monitor the outcomes of youth after they leave care.

Chapter Two: The transition from state care to adulthood: International examples of best practices

Carrie Reid

Around the world, the transition from adulthood is a difficult time for many youth. It is even more difficult for those who are transitioning to adulthood without the benefit of a support network full of family and friends. Youth leaving state care face a transition to independence and adulthood without many of the skills and supports most others take for granted. Preparedness is key to a successful transition, and youth leaving state care tend to be lacking it. In order for youth to truly be prepared for the transition process, they must have support in key areas of their lives: relationships, education, housing, life skills, identity, youth engagement, emotional healing, and adequate financial support. Without these supports, the dismal outcomes for youth transitioning to adulthood will remain unchanged. The United States, England, and Australia have successful programs targeting youth as they transition out of state care. These initiatives bring together and address the variety of needs of this unique population and aim to improve outcomes. While many of these programs and policies are in their infancy, they show promising results, and each contributes valuable experience to successfully working with youth through this tough transition.

Chapter Three: The role of housing in the transition process of youth and young adults: A twenty-year perspective
Mark J. Kroner

Lighthouse Youth Services in Cincinnati, Ohio, began placing foster youth, ages sixteen to eighteen, in individual apartments and other living arrangements in 1981 as a way of preparing them for life after foster care. The program has assisted over thirteen hundred youth and their children using scattered-site apartments, shared homes, roommate situations, host homes, and subsidized housing. The agency works with referring agencies to develop a transition plan one youth at a time and allows youth to move along a continuum of housing options depending on their level of functioning and behavior. Aftercare services assist youth for years after they leave custody. This chapter includes some case studies and summarizes the author's observations from running the program for the past twenty years.

Chapter Four: Transition without status: The experience of youth leaving care without Canadian citizenship
Francis G. Hare

The origins of the project reviewed in this chapter lie in discussions with a Toronto agency that has a mandate to serve youth in transition from the care of the Children's Aid Society. This service system, also known in various jurisdictions as child welfare, child protection, or foster care, includes among its clients children and youth who are living in Canada without legal Canadian status. This could have occurred because the child arrived alone and was taken into care on arrival or because the child arrived with a family but was taken into care before status was obtained. While the child is in care, this lack of status is relatively inconsequential in that health, educational, and other services are provided through the Children's Aid Societies. Once the transition is made from care, the youth's vulnerability increases dramatically if legal status has not been obtained. Health services, educational opportunities, and legal employment are often beyond reach, and the youth is subject to deportation. The major objectives of the project were to explore the national and international literature to discover the dimensions of this issue, interview youth and service providers to gain insight into their experience, and discover ways to minimize the number of youth who leave care without having obtained status.

Chapter Five: Promoting autonomous functioning among youth in care: A program evaluation

Martin Goyette

Over the past few years, considerable research has highlighted the challenges posed by social reinsertion of youth. For youth who leave an alternative living environment at the outset of adulthood, this integration is all the more difficult on account of psychosocial and health factors and a lack of support in preparing for independent living and employment requirements. Although they possess various qualifications and resources for making this difficult transition, many find themselves relying on public-funded services as they enter adulthood. After a brief outline of the contextual organization of youth protection offered in Quebec, the author presents an intervention program that aims to prepare youth in high-risk categories for social reintegration and independent living. This is followed by a presentation of preliminary results stemming from a three-year pilot study and an outline for intervention and support for troubled youths who are entering adulthood.

Chapter Six: Juvenile offenders and independent living: An Irish perspective on program development with St. Xavier's

Niall McElwee, Michael O'Connor, Susan McKenna

This chapter views a specific population within the Irish social care system and draws from the authors' collective experience in relation to young offenders who are leaving care. It describes how effective program development for these youth is considered crucial to their long-term success and permeates all good practice.

Chapter Seven: The Scottish perspective: A pathway to progress?

Jeremy Millar

This chapter provides a historical overview of the development of care and aftercare practices in Scotland. It highlights significant developments in legislation and social policy and offers a critical analysis that draws on the author's experience as a practitioner.

Chapter Eight: Using youth expertise at all levels: The essential resource for effective child welfare practice

Kathi M. Crowe

This chapter highlights the importance of ensuring that youth are partners in every aspect of service planning at individual and program levels. The author outlines this significant and recent development in the field of transitional living services and provides recommendations for meaningful youth involvement at both the micro and the macro levels.

Former youth in care show a disturbing pattern of poor outcomes after they leave the child welfare system. What can be done to promote more successful transitions?

1

Youth leaving care: How do they fare?

Anne Tweddle

THIS CHAPTER LOOKS AT RECENT Canadian, American, and international research on what happens to youth who age out of the child welfare system. The findings show a consistently disturbing pattern of poor outcomes for youth leaving foster care.

In September 2005, the Toronto-based Task Force on Modernizing Income Security for Working Age Adults (MISWAA) examined Canada's income security system and presented proposals to improve the economic security of low-income, working-age adults. Former youth in care, with their poor outcomes and limited prospects for self-sufficiency as they progress through adulthood, are a small but important part of this population. In Canada, provincial and territorial governments have the jurisdictional responsibility for child welfare. In all provinces and territories, this responsibility ends when the youth reaches the age of majority, generally eighteen. Youth in care may receive extended services past age eighteen, subject to certain requirements.

This chapter is a summary of a 2005 briefing paper prepared for the Toronto-based Task Force on Modernizing Income Security for Working Age Adults. Funding was provided by the Laidlaw Foundation.

Nationally, the number of children coming into care has been increasing over the past fifteen years. It is estimated that in March 2003, eighty-five thousand children were in the care of provincial, territorial, and First Nations agencies.[1] Although data are not available on the number of youth who age out of the child welfare system, we do know that they face many more challenges than their peers.

Youth leaving care do not have a family support network, they have limited or no financial resources, they are often lacking in life skills, they usually have not completed school, they often suffer from low self-esteem, and they bear emotional scars from the trauma of childhood neglect or abuse.[2] Once on their own, they are at much greater risk of becoming homeless, engaging in substance abuse, becoming single parents, relying on social assistance, or coming into contact with the criminal justice system. Yet we expect them to fend for themselves when they reach eighteen.

Canadian research

There has been limited Canadian research on what happens to youth when they leave the child welfare system.

Martin studied twenty-nine former youth in care who had turned eighteen years old in 1994.[3] She found that two-thirds were still in high school yet none had completed high school, 38 percent received welfare, 50 percent of the females were mothers and 38 percent of all participants were parents, 7 percent were in jail at the time of the interview (over half had been in jail since leaving care), and 90 percent had moved in the previous year.

Some youth, regardless of their past and ongoing challenges, are remarkably resilient and appear to have more positive outcomes as they progress through the child welfare system and move toward independence and adulthood. Silva-Wayne examined resilience in children and youth in care.[4] She studied nineteen successful child welfare graduates in Ontario, ranging in age from sixteen to twenty-six years. These individuals were working or in school or were parents, had a permanent address, had one significant person in their lives, and had a social network and a positive self-image. She found that their transitions were more successful because they had role models and pathfinders to help them reach their goals, were involved in group activities, had developed a positive self-image through supportive relationships, were exposed to opportunities, and were self-reliant and assertive.

The University of Victoria is midway through its Promoting Positive Outcomes for Youth From Care Project, a prospective, longitudinal study that aims "to better understand the processes, supports and resources that make a positive difference to youth and that help to lead to successful transitions from care."[5] Researchers are following thirty-seven youths formerly in foster care for two-and-one-half years after they leave care. In March 2006, the results of the second interviews were released.[6] The key findings were:

- Transience was common (30 percent reported they had moved four or more times within eighteen months of leaving care).
- Over one-third were on income (social) assistance.
- Nearly one-third were parents.
- One-half were concerned about their physical health.
- One-quarter were concerned about their mental health (half reported they suffered from depression).

The youth also indicated that along with the loss of supportive relationships, financial hardship was the most difficult aspect of leaving care.

International research

There are many international studies on the outcomes of youth who have left care. Although the approaches taken vary considerably, certain common characteristics of former youth in care emerge. These youth are:

- More likely to be undereducated; many have not completed high school
- More likely to be unemployed or underemployed
- When employed, more likely to have low earnings, with many living below the poverty line
- More likely to become a parent at a younger age
- More likely to be incarcerated or involved in the criminal justice system
- More likely to experience homelessness
- More likely to live in an unstable housing arrangement
- More likely to be dependent on social assistance
- More likely to have mental health issues
- More likely not to have medical insurance (in the United States)
- At higher risk for substance abuse

A detailed summary of the findings from various studies is presented in Table 1.1.

Stein's research on the resilience of youth who have been in care in the United Kingdom points to stable placements, a positive sense of identity, a positive school experience, strong social networks, and preparation for independent living through opportunities for planning and problem solving as being associated with better outcomes for youth once they leave care.[7]

In both the United States and the United Kingdom, much of the recent programming focus for youth leaving care has been on supported independent living programs. The United Kingdom introduced the Children (Leaving Care) Act in 2000. This legislation, which amended the 1989 Children Act, extends the maximum age for government responsibility for children in care from sixteen to eighteen years and provides for greater mandatory supports for youth aged eighteen to twenty-one. The act focuses on education, training, and financial needs. It also provides for personal advisers for youth up to age twenty-one, needs assessments, and the development of pathway plans (that is, independent living plans) to assist in transitional planning. In addition, educational support may be extended to age twenty-four.

Table 1.1. Selected research findings on youth who have left school

	Did not complete high school	Unemployed/ no job experience	Pregnant/ unwed parent	Homeless	On public assistance	Incarcerated	Emotional/ mental health problems	Drug abuse problem	Other
Canadian benchmarks for general population	15% (1995)[a]	13.8% (2003)[b]	6.4% (2000)[c] (c)	NA[d]	5.5% (2003–total population)[e]	1.8%[f]	18% (mental health issues or substance dependency)[g,h]	8% in past 12 months (2002)[g]	
Westat study[1]	66%	61%	17%				38%	17%	• 58% had three or more placements
Westat follow-up study[2] (2.5–4 years after leaving care)	50%	50%	60% (among females)	25% (for at least 1 night)	30%				• Fewer than 20% were self-supporting • One-third had moved five or more times since discharge • Only 40% were employed for one year
University of Wisconsin[3] (12–18 months after leaving care)	37%	39% unemployed when interviewed		12% (at least once since discharge)	• 40% of females • 23% of males	18% (since discharge)			• Access to medical care a problem for 44% due to lack of health insurance • Half received mental health services while in care but only 20% did after discharge • Job retention was problem *(continues on next page)*

Table 1.1. continued

	Did not complete high school	Unemployed/ no job experience	Pregnant/ unwed parent	Homeless	On public assistance	Incarcerated	Emotional/ mental health problems	Drug abuse problem	Other
Wisconsin study of Unemployment and Social Assistance[4] (youth exiting care 1992–1998)		• 21% unemployed • 24% sporadically employed (left 1995–1997)			26% (3–5 years after leaving care)				• Youth discharged from foster homes earned more than those discharged from institutions • Earnings much lower than full-time minimum wage earnings • Youth of color less likely to be employed • Median earnings plus assistance was $2,850
Nevada KIDS COUNT[5] (6 months after leaving care)	• 50% on leaving care • 37% at time of interview	37% at time of interview	38%	37%		41%			• 41% couldn't cover basic expenses • 60% earned under $10,000 and 34% less than $5,000 in 1999 • 24% had dealt drugs • 11% engaged in prostitution • 41% in violent relationships • 55% had no health insurance

California study[6]	37–55%	25–51%	40–60%	10–35%	32–47%	18–42%	• All earnings below the 1997 poverty line. • Average earnings were $6,000 per year
University of Chicago study[7]		• Up to 30% unemployed • Up to 45% underemployed				
University of Illinois, Foster Youth in Transition[8] (Phase 2) (2–3 years postdischarge at age 21)	30%	51%			43% of females	• One-third were employed full time • Average annual income was $4,100 (1994–1995) • 90% of females earned less than $10,000 • Only 10% of females had health/medical insurance
Univ. of Illinois - Foster Youth in Transition[8] (Phase 3) (9–10 years post discharge at age 28)	8% at time of interview					• All had improved their situation • 27% of females earned less than $10,000 • 70% of females had health or medical insurance • males fared better, with only 8% earning <$10,000 *(continues on next page)*

Table 1.1. continued

	Did not complete high school	Unemployed/ no job experience	Pregnant/ unwed parent	Homeless	On public assistance	Incarcerated	Emotional/ mental health problems	Drug abuse problem	Other
Casey Northwest Foster Care Alumni Study[9] (in care, 1988–1998)	16%	20% (excludes full-time students and homemakers)	22.5% had children (32% of females and 13% of males)	22% since discharge	17% at time of interview and 48% over past 6 months		55% in previous 12 months		• 33% had incomes below poverty line • 33% had no health insurance
Midwest Evaluation of the Adult Functioning of Former Foster Youth (2005): WAVE TWO[10] (results based on those who had left care unless noted otherwise)	36% had not completed high school or received GED	53% were unemployed at time of interview, and 72% worked during last year. Of these, nearly 75% earned less than $5,000		14% had been homeless since discharge	39% received government assistance since first interview: 25% were currently in receipt of benefits (total sample)	33% arrested since first interview	33% (total sample)		• Study looked at 19-year-old foster youths, some still in care and some who had left care (53% of sample were no longer in care) • Findings are compared to 19 year olds from the National Longitudinal Study of Adolescent Health
Australian study[11] (left care Feb.–Sept. 1996)	Less than 20% completed high school	64% unemployed or on supporting parents benefit	33% of women	50% since discharge					• 50% had committed criminal offense since discharge

| United Kingdom[12] | 75% (no academic qualifications) | 50% | 17% on leaving care | 30% | 38% young prisoners |

Sources:
For Canadian benchmarks:

[a]1995 School Leavers Follow-Up Survey, youth aged 24 years. (http://www11.hrsdc.gc.ca/en/cs/sp/hrsdc/1998-000023/page07.shtml)

[b]Statistics Canada, youth aged 15–24 years. (http://www.statcan.ca/english/freepub/82-221-XIE/2004002/tables/html/2242_02.htm)

[c]Statistics Canada, single parents aged 15–24 as percentage of all single parents. (http://www.statcan.ca/english/freepub/89-575-XIE/89-575-XIE2001001.pdf)

[d]National Homelessness Secretariat. (http://www.homelessness.gc.ca/homelessness/h02_e.asp)

[e]National Council of Welfare, total welfare recipients as of March 2003. (http://www.ncwcnbes.net/htmdocument/principales/numberwelfare_e.htm) and Statistics Canada population estimates for 2003 (http://www.statcan.ca/Daily/English/041221/d041221e.htm)

[f]Juristat, Catalogue 85-002, Vol. 22 #9: Recidivism among convicted youth and young adults, 1999–2000. Youth aged 18–25 years. (http://www.statcan.ca/english/preview/85-002-XIE/P0090285-002-XIE.pdf) and Statistics Canada Census population data, by single years of age (2001) (http://www12.statcan.ca/english/census01/products/standard/themes/RetrieveProductTable.cfm?Temporal=2001&PID=55437&APATH=3&GID=431515&METH=1&PTYPE=55430&THEME=37&FOCUS=0&AID=0&PLACENAME=0&PROVINCE=0&SEARCH=0&GC=0&GK=0&VID=0&FL=0&RL=0&FREE=0)

[g]Canadian Community Health Survey: Mental health and well-being, 2002 (http://www.statcan.ca/Daily/English/030903/d030903a.htm)

[h]*Winnipeg Free Press* article, September 13, 2003 (http://www.cpa.ca/documents/WFP2.pdf)

Casey Family Programs, Outcomes for Youth Exiting Foster Care, June 2001 (items 1–5 inclusive)

[i]Westat study—focus on youth who emancipated from foster care between January 1987 and July 1988 (Cook, 1990). Total sample: 800 youth.

(continues on next page)

[2] Westat follow-up study of youth who emancipated from foster care between January 1987 and July 1988 2.5–4 years after leaving care (Cook, 1992). Total sample: 113 youth. Cook, R. (1990). *A national evaluation of Title IV-E Foster Care Independent Living Programs for Youth*, phase I. Rockville, MD: Westat.

[3] University of Wisconsin—study of youth 12–18 months after they emancipated from foster care in 1995. Courtney, M. E., & Piliavin, I. (1998). *Foster youths transitions to adulthood: Outcomes 12 to 18 months after leaving out-of-home care*. Madison: School of Social Work, University of Wisconsin–Madison.

[4] Dworsky and Courtney, Wisconsin—unemployment insurance wage data and public assistance data of youth who exited foster care 1992–1998. Dworsky, A., & Courtney, M. E. (2000). *Self-sufficiency of former foster youth in Wisconsin: Analysis of unemployment insurance wage data and public assistance data*. (http://aspe.hhs.gov/hsp/fosteryouthWI00).

[5] Nevada KIDS COUNT—study of 100 youth who emancipated from care 6 or more months ago, 2001, University of Nevada.

[6] 1999 Little Hoover Commission Report, *Now in Our Hands: Caring for California's Abused & Neglected Children*. Data from brief at http://www.emq.org/press/issue_fostercare.html.

[7] University of Chicago. *Employment Outcomes for Youth Aging of Foster Care*, March 2002. Children leaving care in the mid-1990s in California, Illinois and South Carolina. http://aspe.hhs.gov/search/hsp/fostercare-agingout02/

[8] Foster Youth in Transition, University of Illinois, Phases 1 and 2, from Mech, E. V. (2003). *Uncertain futures: Foster youth in transition to adulthood*. Washington, DC: CWLA Press.

[9] The Northwest Foster Care Alumni Study, Casey Family Programs, 2005. Sample of 479 foster care alumni who were in care between 1988 and 1998. http://www.casey.org/NR/rdonlyres/4E1E7C77-7624-4260-A253-892C5A6CB9E1/300/nw_alumni_study_full_apr2005.pdf

[10] Midwest Evaluation of the Adult Functioning of Former Foster Youth, Chapin Hall Centre for Children, May 2005. Wave two of longitudinal study of foster youth interviewed between March and December 2004. Sample for second wave was 602 youth, 282 of whom were still in care and 321 who had left care. http://www.chapinhall.org/article_abstract.aspx?ar=1355.

[11] *Young people leaving care and protection: A report to the National Youth Affairs Research Scheme*, Australian Clearinghouse for Youth Studies http://www.acys.utas.edu.au/nyars/N17_exec.htm.

[12] U.K. House of Commons Research Paper 00/63, June 2000, page 8 (http://www.parliament.uk/commons/lib/research/rp2000/rp00-063.pdf).

The United States passed the Foster Care Independence Act in 1999, replacing the Title IV-E Independent Living Initiative of 1986. The new legislation doubled the available federal funds for transitional assistance for children between the ages of eighteen and twenty-one who are preparing to age out or who have aged out of the foster care system. One of the results of the act was to create the John H. Chafee Foster Care Independence Program, which emphasizes independent living services with a focus on education, employment, and life skills training. It provides for room and board for foster children out of care who are less than twenty-one years of age. It also encourages states to provide former youth in care aged eighteen to twenty-one with Medicaid coverage.

One of the requirements of the act is the establishment of the National Youth-in-Transition Database to assess the outcomes of youth. The U.S. Department of Health and Human Services was directed to develop outcome measures to assess states' independent living programs. The measures are to focus on educational attainment, employment and labor force participation, and avoidance of social assistance dependency, unwed child birth, homelessness, contact with the correctional system, and incarceration. As of early 2007, the database had not been implemented.

A 2004 brief by the U.S. organization Voices for America's Children highlights the lack of in-depth research on children aging out of foster care.[8] It points to three promising studies: the Casey National Alumni Study, the Multi-Site Evaluation of Foster Youth Programs, and the Midwest Evaluation of Adult Functioning of Former Foster Youth: Conditions of Youth Preparing to Leave State Care.

The Casey National Alumni Study examines alumni who had been in foster care between 1966 and 1998 (the sample size was 1,609). Preliminary results identified the following areas as good predictors of successful outcomes:[9]

- Completion of high school while in care
- Access to postsecondary opportunities
- Life skills and independent living training
- Not being homeless within one year of leaving care

- Participation in clubs while in care
- Minimal academic problems
- Minimal use of alcohol or drugs

The Multi-Site Evaluation of Foster Youth Programs will evaluate programs funded by the John Chafee Foster Care Independence Program over a five-year period. Four programs are being evaluated: employment services program (California), intensive case management/mentoring program (Massachusetts), tutoring/mentoring program (California), and life skills training program (California). Results are forthcoming.

The Midwest Evaluation of Adult Functioning of Former Foster Youth: Conditions of Youth Preparing to Leave State Care examined 732 youth in Iowa, Illinois, and Wisconsin between the ages of seventeen and twenty-one. Wave 2, which focuses on findings at age nineteen, shows these youth to be at a considerable disadvantage when compared to their peers. Selected findings are included in Table 1.1.

Initiatives under way in Canada

Participants at the February 2003 Canadian Symposium on Child and Family Services Outcomes noted that there had been limited progress on research on the effectiveness of interventions and the tracking of outcomes.[10] The two research activities under way in Canada that focus on child welfare outcomes are the Child Welfare Outcome Study (Bell Canada Child Welfare Research Centre) and the Canadian version of Looking After Children (CanLAC).

The Child Welfare Outcome Study focuses on measuring child welfare outcomes in four domains: child safety, child well-being, permanence, and family and community supports.[11] The Child Welfare Outcome Indicator Matrix, developed in the late 1990s, identifies ten indicators within these four domains: recurrence of maltreatment, serious injury or death, school performance, child behavior, placement rate, moves in care, time to achieving permanent placement, family moves, parenting capacity, and ethnocultural placement matching. The indicators are proxy measures based on data available from provincial information systems. The system was pilot-tested across Canada in 2001 and is being assessed to determine its ability to report national data.

CanLAC is the Canadian version of Looking After Children (LAC).[12] LAC, which was developed and field-tested in Great Britain between 1987 and 1995, focuses on clinical outcomes for children in care in order to assess the child's needs and progress. It measures a child's development in seven key domains—health, education, identity, family and social relationships, social presentation, emotional and behavioral development, and self-care skills—by means of an annual questionnaire. Information is gathered through a series of action and assessment records that chart a child's progress while in care and measures his or her progress toward clearly identified goals. Most Canadian jurisdictions are using CanLAC in varying capacities.

Although these outcome measures are useful tools while children are in care, neither is designed to monitor outcomes for youth once they leave care.

In 2004, the province of Alberta implemented its Youth in Transition initiative.[13] Youth transitioning from care are an important component of the initiative. The province is developing an exit survey for children in care.

A number of initiatives provide opportunities for youth leaving care to pursue their education. In Ontario, the University of Toronto's Transitional Year Programme assists many youth who have been in care by offering a one-year program to assist them in developing the skills and attitudes needed to succeed in a university environment.[14] Alberta's Advancing Futures Bursary program is for former youth who were in care for a minimum of eighteen month and are between the ages of sixteen and twenty-two years.[15] The bursary provides for tuition, books, school expenses, and living expenses for youth who meet the entrance requirements. The new Canada Learning Bond is designed to help low-income families (including children in care) with the cost of postsecondary education.[16] The federal government contributes five hundred dollars for each child born on or after January 1,

2004, and one hundred dollars each year until the child reaches fifteen years of age. The bond is paid into a registered education savings plan.

Future directions

The importance of appropriate service planning for children and youth while they are in care is well recognized. Studies have shown the negative effects of numerous placement changes, school change, and nonsupportive relationships on eventual outcomes once these youth leave care.

Canadian youth who have aged out of the child welfare system have consistently and clearly identified what types of services and resources they need to assist them in their transition from care.[17] They have spoken of their frustration of being cut off from the system once they reach their eighteenth birthday to fend for themselves, with limited life skills, financial support, and support networks. In most cases, they say they were not emotionally ready to live independently. In order to ensure a more successful transition to adulthood, youth leaving care say they need:

- Increased access to, and availability of, financial support
- Ongoing supportive relationships during their transition from care and afterward
- Mentoring and peer support
- Individualized support and mechanisms for the transition and posttransition periods
- Support in gaining access to education, employment, and training programs
- Independent living training
- Opportunities to develop decision-making and problem-solving skills

In order to improve the outcomes for youth as they leave the child welfare system for independent living, governments need to improve their transitional planning for these young people who are approaching the age of majority. To this end, governments should:

- Ensure the availability of extended services (including health benefits) and financial assistance to youth up to age twenty-four
- Ensure that the amount of financial assistance is sufficient to cover living costs and incorporate an annual indexation provision
- Ensure that mandatory standards are in place to prepare youth for leaving care
- Ensure that there is a regular review process for all youth receiving extended services
- Explore financial options to enable youth in care to pursue higher education or training, which could include tuition waivers, scholarships, grants, or the conversion of student loans to grants for youth in care

In the long term, Canadian governments need to develop a national longitudinal survey to monitor the outcomes of youth after they leave care. Governments should also commit to researching organizations to identify which interventions and models result in the best outcomes for youth leaving care.

Governments want evidence-based research and outcome measures to justify new program and policy directions. Researchers, meanwhile, emphasize that there are no data pointing to which programs best serve youth as they make the transition from the child welfare system. Clearly, tools need to be developed and implemented to generate data on outcomes as youth make the transition into adulthood and identify what interventions result in more successful outcomes.

Notes

1. Tweddle, A. (2005). Estimated based on data from Social Development Canada and Indian and Northern Affairs Canada. These data are based on five separate studies: (1) Cook, R. (1990). *A national evaluation of Title IV-E Foster Care Independent Living Programs for Youth, phase I*. Rockville, MD: Westat. (2) Cook, R. (1992). *A national evaluation of Title IV-E Foster Care Independent Living Programs for Youth, phase II*. Rockville, MD: Westat. (3) Courtney, M. E., & Piliavin, I. (1998). *Foster youths' transitions to adulthood: Outcomes 12–18*

months after leaving out-of-home care. Madison: School of Social Work, University of Wisconsin-Madison. (4) Dworsky, A., & Courtney, M. E. (2000). *Self-sufficiency of former foster youth in Wisconsin: Analysis of unemployment insurance wage data and public assistance data.* Available at http://aspe.hhs.gov./hsp/fosteryouthW100/. (5) Nevada Kids COUNT. (2001). *Transition from care: The status and outcomes of youth who have aged out of the foster care system in Clark County, Nevada.* Las Vegas: University of Nevada.

2. Raychaba, B. (1988). *To be on our own with no direction from home: A report on the special needs of youth leaving the care of the child welfare system.* Ottawa: National Youth in Care Network.

3. Martin, F. (1996). Tales of transition: Leaving public care. In J. Hudson & B. Galaway (Eds.), *Youth in transition: Perspectives on research and policy* (pp. 99–106). Toronto: Thompson Educational Publishing.

4. Silva-Wayne, S. (1995). Contributions to resilience in children and youth: What successful child welfare graduates say. In J. Hudson & B. Galaway (Eds.), *Child welfare in Canada: Research and policy implications* (pp. 308–323). Toronto: Thompson Educational Publishing.

5. Rutman, D., Hubberstey, C., Barlow, A., & Brown, E. (2005). *Promoting positive outcomes for youth from care: When Youth Age Out of Care Project: A report on baseline findings.* August 2005. Retrieved May 2006 from http://socialwork.uvic.ca/research/projects.htm.

6. Rutman et al. (2005).

7. Stein, M. (2005). Resilience and young people leaving care: Implications for child welfare policy and practice in the UK. In R. J. Flynn, P. M. Dudding, & J. G. Barber (Eds.), *Promoting resilience in child welfare* (pp. 264–278). Ottawa: University of Ottawa Press.

8. Dunne, L. (2004). *Effective approaches to supporting youth aging out of foster care.* Retrieved June 2004 from http://www.voicesforamericaschildren.org/Content/ContentGroups/Policy/Child_Safety/Member_Mailing1/Supporting_Youth_Aging_Out_of_Foster_Care_What_Does_the_Research_Tell_Us_/issue_brief_8–04_c.pdf.

9. Pecora, P., Williams, J., Kessler, R., Downs, A., O'Brien, K., Hiripi, E., & Morello, S. (2003). *Assessing the effects of foster care: Early results from the Casey National Alumni Study.* Retrieved June 2005 from http://www.casey.org/Resources/Publications/NationalAlumniStudy.htm.

10. Canadian Outcomes Research Institute. (2003). *Canadian Symposium of Child and Family Services Outcomes.* Calgary, Alberta: Author.

11. Trocmé, N., Nutter, B., MacLaurin, B., & Fallon, B. (1999). *Child welfare outcome indicator matrix.* Retrieved June 2005 from http://www.cecw-cepb.ca/DocsEng/OutcomesIndicatorMatrix.pdf.

12. Canadian Looking After Children Project. Retrieved June 2005 from http://www.cwlc.ca/projects/canlac_e.htm.

13. Youth in Transition Policy Framework. (2001). Retrieved June 2005 from http://www.child.gov.ab.ca/whoweare.

14. Transitional Year Programme. Retrieved June 2005 from http://www.library.utoronto.ca/typ/.

15. Advancing Futures: A bursary program for youth in government care. Retrieved June 2005 from http://www.child.gov.ab.ca/whoweare.
16. Canada Learning Bond. (2004). Press release. Retrieved June 2005 from http://www.hrsdc.gc.ca/en/cs/comm/hrsd/news/2004/041008.shtml.
17. Raychaba. (1988); Rutman, D., Strega, S., Callahan, M., & Dominelli, L. (2001). Young Mothers In/From Care Project: Proceedings of the April 3, 2001, Forum on Policy and Practice. Retrieved June 2005 from http://www.cecw-cepb.ca; Martin, F., & Palmer, T. (1997). *Transitions to adulthood: A youth perspective.* Ottawa, Canada: Child Welfare League of Canada.

ANNE TWEDDLE *recently retired from the federal civil service, where she worked in the field of Canadian social programs, with a special focus on social assistance and child welfare. Since her retirement, she has worked for the Toronto City Summit Alliance and St. Christopher House Task Force on Modernizing Income Security for Working-Age Adults and the National Council of Welfare.*

Youth who are moving out of state care require a number of important supports to aid in their successful transition to adulthood. Without these, they lack the proper tools and risk limited life chances.

2

The transition from state care to adulthood: International examples of best practices

Carrie Reid

THE ISSUE OF OUTCOMES for youth who transition from state care to adulthood is not unique to any one country. Youth exiting the child welfare system, or aging out, face a plethora of problems and issues associated with the transition to adulthood. Research from countries all over the world say the same thing about youth leaving the child welfare system: compared to their peers, youth aging out of care are more likely to leave school before completing their secondary education; become a parent at a young age; be dependent on social assistance; be unemployed or underemployed; be incarcerated or otherwise involved with the criminal justice system; experience homelessness; have mental health problems; and be at higher risk for substance abuse problems.[1] The similarities across regions and countries beg the question, What will help youth more successfully transition to adulthood?

For the majority of youth, the transition to adulthood represents a process that takes place over a period of time with the support of family and friends. In Canada and around the rest of the world, it is becoming commonplace for youth to depend on their parents well into their twenties.[2] Research shows that the age of leaving home has steadily increased over the past decade.[3] Intergenerational interdependence is the norm in most societies. Youth in state care are considered at risk, yet they are the ones most unlikely to be receiving support from family or the state.[4] They do not have a sturdy safety net to catch them as they waiver on the brink of adulthood.

Research shows that relationships, education, housing, life skills, identity, youth engagement, and emotional healing are key areas that help determine how successful a youth is likely to be in the transition process.[5] These seven pillars are built on a foundation of strong financial support that enables the necessary social supports to be both predictable and sustainable. It is important to understand that these pillars are interdependent; none stands alone as the key area to help ensure better outcomes. Only when all seven areas are examined and addressed with equal vigor and determination will the outcomes for youth improve.

Purpose

The original purpose of this chapter was to explore why youth aging out of the Canadian child welfare system do not fare as well as their peers. The issue was made even more urgent with the 2006 release of a documentary, *Wards of the Crown*, by Canadian filmmaker Andrée Cazabon. The Centre of Excellence in Child Welfare, along with the Child Welfare League of Canada and the National Youth in Care Network, came together to produce a paper that would raise awareness among government officials, caregivers, frontline staff, managers, and community members about the needs of youth transitioning out of the child welfare system. The seven pillars and foundation were drawn from national and international research and particularly from programs and policies that undertook to address multiple issues to meet the goal of better outcomes for youth exiting state care. It became clear that there are initiatives under way across the world designed to improve outcomes and challenge contemporary thinking on what these youth need to succeed.

This chapter explores international initiatives in the context of the seven pillars and foundation. Each pillar is briefly outlined, followed by an exploration of international policies, programs, and legislation in place to address the issue of youth leaving care. The United States, United Kingdom, and Australia are used as key examples because each is unique in the context of its political, social, and economic systems, but they share the common feature of demonstrating what best practices can look like.

Given the international focus here, a definition of children and youth in state care is necessary. Some countries may include those involved in the juvenile justice or the mental health systems as in state care.[6] However, for the purposes of this chapter, only children and youth who are placed in out-of-home care and are in need of protection are included in the definition of those in state care. As well, it is generally understood that aging out of the care system occurs in late adolescence but ranges in age depending on the jurisdiction.[7] The actual chronological age is less important than the programs in place to facilitate the transition.

Seven pillars and the foundation

When thinking about the seven pillars and foundation for success for youth aging out of care, it is difficult to know where to start. No one area can be discussed without touching on the importance of the others. The areas of relationships, education, housing, life skills, identity, youth engagement, emotional healing, and financial support are the major issues facing youth transitioning out of care. It is imperative that each of these areas be seen as only a part of the explanation. As a whole, they provide a complete picture.

Relationships

The importance of relationships to human development cannot be stressed enough. No one needs to read academic research to understand that people need love and affection, support, and people they can count on in good times and bad. Unfortunately for children and youth in the child welfare system, long-term and meaningful relationships are hard to come by. Trust in adults is often damaged because of past experiences, frequent moves, separation from family, and a myriad of other factors that contribute to the lack of long-term and meaningful relationships in the lives of children and youth leaving care.[8] A positive and trusting relationship with an adult or an external support system plays an important role in helping youth overcome challenges.[9] Children need to be encouraged by peers and adults in order to feel a sense of accomplishment and belonging.[10] Without these feelings, children become disengaged and lack the resources necessary for success. Research shows that youth who maintain relationships with at least one important adult are far more likely go on to have successful outcomes.[11] Thus, a key factor for the success of youth leaving care is the same as what all other youth need: an adult who cares and provides support in good times and bad.

Education

High school graduation is an expectation for the majority of youth. Without a high school diploma, the likelihood of finding employment lessens, and the employment that can be found is often low skilled and even lower paying. We live in a knowledge-based society where education, literacy, and numeracy are essential.[12] For youth in care, completing high school can be both a dream and a nightmare. How do youth focus on school when they have to look for a place to live or work to make ends meet? Education attainment for youth in care is not simply completing high school. Reaching that milestone for many is a huge accomplishment, but many obstacles stand in the way. Roadblocks are present throughout the education process, not simply at the point of graduation.[13] Youth leaving the child welfare system are often referred to as *grad-*

uates, and they become alumni. But when the only graduation many can discuss is their graduation from the child welfare system and not high school, they have a vulnerability with potentially lifelong consequences.

Level of education is one of the best indicators for future success.[14] It can be measured in any number of ways, from employment status and income to lifestyle. Regardless of what is being measured and how, education is an important step to achieving goals. Despite this well-known fact, youth in care consistently graduate at rates significantly lower than their peers.[15] Many factors combine to work against youth. Children taken into care lack stability in all aspects of their lives. With each placement change comes the likelihood of a new school, new teachers, new curriculum, and new uncertainty. The system is not designed for children to bounce between schools at any time during the school year and still be able to fit in with both the students and the lesson plans. Addressing the unique educational needs of youth in care, during their stay in state care and their transition out of it, will help give these youth the skills they need in adulthood.

Housing

Having a place to call home is a distant dream for many youth in care. For some in the child welfare system, the transient lifestyle of moving from placement to placement is a reality with impacts on all aspects of their life.[16] From education disruptions and loss of significant relationships to a sense of not belonging anywhere, this lack of stability forms the basis for life in care. It is not uncommon for youth to change their placements once a year, more if the youth is deemed to be "trouble."[17] These placements can be foster homes, group homes, or other facilities designed to serve the complex needs of children and youth in the child welfare system. What many people do not think about is that with each change of home comes a loss of relationships and often a disruption to education. With the scarcity of resources in which to place youth, location and minimal disruption to the youth are secondary to having a place to tell the youth is home.

The impacts of moving on education and relationships aside, the detrimental effects of never knowing where to call home and for how long they will be welcome is emotionally damaging to youth. They are constantly living in homes to which they have no real stake, possibly with families that they feel may reject them at any time or in group homes where misbehavior can result in eviction. Teenagers living at home with their family do not have to worry about finding a new place to live if they miss curfew once too often or have a temper tantrum because they did not get their way. The fragility of a placement is reinforced when those in authority respond to problem behaviors with a caution about a potential placement change. It may seem to have a positive impact in the short term, but there are long-term potential consequences for the youth's sense of stability and could possibly inflict further trauma.[18]

Life skills

The placement and relationship histories of youth shape the life skills they have as they transition out of care. When youth have stable home and educational experiences, the life skills that are generally learned through observation and practice are just as innate to youth aging out of the foster care system as they are to almost everyone else. Those people with whom a youth in care has significant relationships can teach skills and encourage the development of others. This gives youth the opportunity to learn, ask questions, and have someone to work with on these skills. Just as transitioning out of care is a process that takes time, so is the process of learning the skills necessary to succeed. These skills take practice, and failures and bumps along the way are to be expected. Youth need to have the time and resources dedicated to ensuring they have the skills necessary to live independently before they are expected to do so.

Identity

All of us have a fundamental right to know who we are and where we come from. Children grow up asking questions about their families, culture, and background. This is normal and to be expected, even of children and youth in the child welfare system. The answers may not be as easy to come by, but that does not mean that the questions should be ignored. It is imperative that every child in state care is given an opportunity to learn, understand, and appreciate his or her history and culture. Furthermore, children and youth need to have their personal identities as individuals as well as members of communities reinforced so that each youth leaves care feeling as though he or she belongs and has a strong sense of self.

Youth engagement

What youth want is the ability to work toward their own future instead of having it imposed on them.[19] Parents of teenagers attest to the fact that you cannot tell a teenager what to do or how to do it, so there is no reason that social workers should think it would be any different for a youth in care. When a youth is able to feel a sense of ownership of the plan for his or her life, the likelihood of the youth's following through and working toward agreed-on goals is remarkably higher than when a youth is simply told what is best and how to do it. Teenagers want to be causal agents in their own lives but to be supported when they make mistakes.[20] Sometimes parents, even when the state acts as parents, have to let go and allow their child to do what he or she is going to do. Youth learn as much from their successes as they do from their failures, and the child welfare system has to allow that. Helping youth learn how to make important decisions is as important as ensuring that they make the right decisions.

Emotional healing

The behaviors of youth can be erratic and destructive. In response, adults may get angry and dole out punishment. The behaviors youth exhibit are not for the sake of acting out, but rather a result of past unhealed trauma. While it often makes sense to discipline a child or youth for behaviors that are antisocial, discipline does not address the reasons for the behavior. If more time were spent addressing what causes the behaviors instead of the punitive responses to the behaviors, youth would be much better off.[21] Affection rather than punishment must be used on youth who exhibit difficult behavior because that is their primary unmet need.[22] Youth need to have the time and resources dedicated to ensuring that their past experiences do not inhibit their future development and success.

The foundation: Financial support

Financial support for youth is a controversial issue, and there is no agreement about what a youth needs and what ought to be provided for. The issue of financial support raises a larger set of questions regarding what level of support is both necessary and reasonable to ensure the full participation of these youth and how the support provided by the child welfare system can be coordinated with other available programs. It is important to establish policy regarding the reasonable level of contribution that young people themselves are expected to make through paid employment, volunteer work, and the assumption of longer-term debt such as student loans. Currently the information on levels of financial support for youth is poorly documented and not readily available. It is important that financial support measures not simply be borrowed from other income security programs, such as general welfare assistance, which are designed for different purposes. Rather, it is necessary to ensure that an inclusive financial support foundation be designed that is flexible and supports the overall objective of aiding a successful transition to adulthood.

International examples

This section outlines notable programs, policies, and legislation in the United States, United Kingdom, and Australia. These examples address the diverse needs of youth leaving care and demonstrate best practices in action.

United States

The following are examples of best practices in the United States.

Casey Family Programs. The Casey Family Programs are foster care and advocacy programs that demonstrate foster care done well.[23] Based in Seattle, Washington, the foundation was established by UPS founder Jim Casey and has served children, youth, and families in the child welfare system since 1966. As a private foster care provider in the United States, its mission is to provide and improve, and ultimately prevent, the need for foster care. This foundation provides direct services and promotes advances in child welfare practice and policy. Through this work, it has produced some remarkable outcomes for children and youth in foster care and helped equip them with the skills and supports to flourish as adults.[24]

This program demonstrates that adequate resources, both financial and human, make a difference in the outcomes for youth. Casey devotes more financial resources than other state agencies, with outcomes to prove the value. The high school graduation rates for youth leaving Casey care are comparable to, if not higher than, the national average high school graduation rate. Over 85 percent of all youth in this program participate in some form of extracurricular activity in sports, the arts, religious organization, or other hobbies.[25] This program shows that youth who are in a program that addresses their many needs are more likely to succeed and have outcomes similar to their peers.

Although many of the outcomes for Casey alumni are promising, more work is needed. Despite the advantages of receiving services from Casey over other agencies, fewer of the alumni who graduated high school go on to postsecondary education than the national average, and the completion rate for postsecondary education is even lower.[26] Despite the areas for improvement in outcomes, Casey Family Programs demonstrate that when youth are supported in all areas of their life, not just one or two, they can more successfully transition out of state care.

Foster Care Independence Act. The U.S. Congress passed the Foster Care Independence Act (FCIA) in November 1999, and it went into effect in 2000, thereby creating the John H. Chafee Foster Care Independence Program. The FCIA considerably increased the opportunities available to youth aging out of care and specifically recognizes the need for permanency planning for older adolescents while also preparing these same youth for independent living. FCIA doubled the amount of federal money available to assist states in providing independent living services, and it focuses on education, employment, and life skills training.[27]

States are required to use at least some portion of their funds to provide follow-up services to foster youth who have already aged out of care. States are allowed to use up to 30 percent of their funds to pay for the room and board of former foster youth between the ages of eighteen and twenty. This ensures that youth at risk of homelessness have support in place to lessen the likelihood of becoming or remaining homeless. FCIA also stipulates that states can give postsecondary educational and training vouchers up to five thousand dollars for youth likely to experience difficulty during the transition to adulthood. States may allow youth participating in the voucher program on their twenty-first birthday to remain eligible until they reach twenty-three years old, with the stipulation that they are enrolled in a postsecondary education or training program and are making satisfactory progress toward completion of that program. Although the current rate of youth continuing on to postsecondary education is relatively low, the financial burden of such an endeavor is lessened with this voucher and can serve as an incentive to complete high school.[28]

United Kingdom

Since the election of the Labour party in 1997, there has been great political support for youth leaving care, and legislative and policy changes reflect this. Local authorities have responsibility for social services, including children in care and care leavers. The central government in London, in partnership with the local authorities, has responsibility for overseeing the well-being of all its citizens. The central government, through the Department of Health, determines the overall direction of policy; the policy is then passed down to the local authorities for implementation and interpretation. The local authorities have some discretion in the implementation of the policies but must maintain a level of consistency.[29]

The Children's Act 1989 previously governed youth leaving care. It indicated that youth were to leave care between the ages of sixteen and eighteen years old. Local authorities had a duty to advise and befriend, as well as a power to assist, youth between sixteen and twenty-one who had left care. This assistance could stretch to age twenty-four for education or training that had begun before the age of twenty-one. The Department of Health recognized that the legislation was not effective and that practices were not sufficient. It conducted research and found that postcare contact was often left to young people to initiate or maintain; most young people were ill informed about available postcare support; few young people had formal care plans; and most local authorities found it difficult to keep track of eighteen to twenty-one year olds.[30]

As a result of these identified problems, the Children (Leaving Care) Act 2000 was created. It ensures that local authorities remain directly responsible for the welfare of their post–age sixteen care leavers until at least age eighteen. There are three major areas of change: benefits, assessment and planning, and the role of personal advisers (an identifiable contact point at the local authority for interaction with social services departments and others who have looked after the youth). Previously, youth aged sixteen and seventeen were entitled to a social security benefit from the central government, so local authorities would encourage youth to leave care and thus reduce their financial burden and shift it onto the central government. Changes to the legislation disallowed sixteen and seventeen year olds to be eligible for this benefit to ensure that local authorities maintain financial and moral responsibility for these youth.[31]

The new legislation requires that adequate planning be done for all youth. A needs assessment must be completed when a future care leaver reaches age sixteen, with the goal of using this plan to aid the leaving-care planning process. These plans must be reviewed at least every six months, which forces the local authorities to keep in touch and meet regularly with youth to discuss their ongoing needs. In addition, a pathway plan is created and is used until the youth is at least twenty-one years old; it identifies the local authority role in meeting the needs of the youth up to that age. However, the local authority is to have a role only where appropriate and necessary in an effort to build self-sufficiency and independence. The role of the local authority is to ensure all gaps in care are filled and support needs are met. This support is provided beyond twenty-one years old and up to age twenty-four years for agreed-on education or training. A notable form of required support is the provision of or support for vacation accommodation while a youth is in postsecondary education.[32]

All care leavers between sixteen and twenty-one years of age have a personal adviser. In addition, all youth aged thirteen to nineteen in England have a connections adviser to provide support on careers and other transitional issues for young people. These advisers are part of a wider agenda for tackling social exclusion among all young people. For youth in care, their connections adviser and leaving-care adviser may be the same person from age sixteen on.[33]

This legislation is effective because it targets core concerns for youth leaving care such as housing, education and employment, finances, and social support with flexible approaches to engage youth in the decision-making processes. The legislation also requires agencies to work cooperatively with each other to meet the needs of youth. However, education and employment outcomes are still poor, and that is likely because the education and training programs for youth older than age sixteen are unable to make up for an earlier lack of stability and support.[34]

Youth leaving care are addressed also through other legislation that can affect relevant areas of a youth's life. A prime example is the Homelessness Act of 2002, which stipulates that priority for services and supports be given to youth who have exited the child welfare system. This highlights an understanding of the reality of life for many youth as they transition out of state care.[35]

Permanency planning through adoption is an important issue in England and Wales. The Adoption and Children Act, passed in 2002, for the first time stated that the best interests of the child are paramount. A driving force behind this legislation was to act as a solution to the problems with the child welfare system, including outcomes from residential care and lack of permanency. There have been significant increases in adoptions from the care system (7 percent in 1975 to 40 percent by the mid-1990s), but this did not do enough to address the issues of children still left in care. Beginning in October 2003, adoptive families were given the right to ask their local authority for adoption support services, which can include financial support. This is discretionary based on the needs of the family and the child.[36]

Australia

Australia has a federal model of government where child protection is the responsibility of the community services department in each state and territory. Each department has its own legislation, policies, and practices in relation to child protection, and there are no uniform in-care or leaving-care standards.[37]

The bulk of children in care in Australia are placed in foster families and with relatives. With only 6 percent of children and youth living outside the traditional forms of alternative care, there have been calls for a broader range of placement options for youth who are not suited to home-based care. Because of this, the Lead Tenant program is being used extensively across the country. The model incorporates features of treatment foster care such as specially recruited and trained caregivers, higher-than-standard caregiver remuneration, intensive placement support, and wraparound services. The client group is youth with at-risk behaviors and complex needs where family-based or institutional care is inappropriate. Typically the program works with two unrelated lead tenants (caregivers) and two youth in the foster home. Most youth complete the program within twelve months. Advantages of the program are reported to be positive role modeling by lead tenants, the development of practical and interpersonal skills and some oversight of outside relationships by the lead tenants.[38]

South Australia has developed a unique model, the Special Youth Career Program (SYC), that incorporates some of the features of treatment foster care and the lead tenant models but differs in several ways:

- Placements are limited to one youth and one caregiver per home.
- The home is not owned by the caregiver.
- A breakdown in the youth-caregiver relationship that cannot be successfully mediated is resolved by replacing the caregiver.

- The program is not time limited.
- On reaching age eighteen, youth may have the option of remaining in the home and assuming legal responsibility for tenancy.[39]

Youth referred to SYC have a history of placement instability, risk taking, or problem behavior or are in crisis and other placement options have been exhausted. Youth who have participated in this program reported feeling a sense of belonging in the SYC home and that it did not feel like a foster placement. This sense of belonging came from their understanding that the SYC home was theirs and not the caregiver's. Having a place to call home did not depend on the goodwill of another. Although this program is in its infancy, initial research is indicating it is a successful alternative to traditional foster care. Not only is the youth supported with wraparound services, the caregiver is also given extensive support to help maintain the stability of the placement. The program appears to be a means of stability of accommodation and continuity of networks and may be effective in reducing high-risk behaviors. These are two very important determinants of successful transition to adulthood. As an interesting aside, the adoption of children and youth in care is rare and not promoted in South Australia, nor is there a provision for the termination of parental rights, meaning there are a lot of youth in foster care and it may not be the best placement option for every one of them. SYC is an excellent alternative model for the most difficult youth.[40]

New South Wales is the only state in Australia to introduce both a legislative and program response for youth leaving care. New South Wales established the statewide After Care Resource Centre, which acts as a resource and advocacy service for young people leaving care or who have left care. All care leavers aged fifteen to twenty-five are able to access these services. However, as of 2004, no official evaluation of the efficacy of these services had been completed so it is difficult to know what impact, if any, this program is having on youth exiting care. As well, a number of other states in Australia have introduced transitional and after-care programs designed to assist care leavers with accommodation and other supports but they tend to be limited and discretionary in nature with no legislative guarantees.[41]

Conclusion

Jurisdictions across the world are working toward bettering outcomes for youth transitioning from state care to adulthood. The programs, policies, and legislation with the most promise of success are those that address the interconnectedness of youth needs. They understand that better outcomes for youth do not involve just an education program or giving the youth more money to ease the transition. No longer is impersonal and minimal the best approach; rather, the most successful programs aim at giving youth the support that any other peer would expect from a parent. Organizations and states are beginning to realize the importance of taking on the role of parent to the children and youth who are legally in their care.

Notes

1. Tweddle, A. (2005). *Youth leaving care—How do they fare?* Briefing paper, Laidlaw Foundation; Munro, E. R., Stein, M., & Ward, H. (2005). Comparing how different social, political and legal frameworks support or inhibit transitions from public care to independence in Europe, Israel, Canada and the United States. *International Journal of Child and Family Welfare, 8*(4), 191–201; Mendes, P., & Moslehuddin, B. (2004). Graduating from the child welfare system: A comparison of the UK and Australian leaving care debates. *International Journal of Social Welfare, 13,* 332–339; Leslie, B., & Hare, F. (2000). Improving the outcomes for youth in transition from care. *Ontario Association of Children's Aid Societies Journal, 44*(3), 19–25.

2. Rutman, D., Hubberstey, C., Barlow, A., & Brown, E. (2005). *When youth age out of care: A report on baseline findings.* Victoria: School of Social Work, University of Victoria.

3. Canadian Council on Social Development. (1996). *The progress of Canada's children 1996.* Ottawa, ON: Canadian Council on Social Development.

4. Munro et al. (2005).

5. See, for example, National Youth in Care Network. (2005). *Current themes facing youth in state care.* Ottawa, ON: National Youth in Care Network; Tweddle. (2005); Rutman et al. (2005); Casey Family Programs (2003). *Assessing the effects of foster care: Early results from the Casey National Alumni Study.* Seattle, WA: Casey Family Programs.

6. Munro et al. (2005).

7. Munro et al. (2005).

8. Collins, M. (2001). Transition to adulthood for vulnerable youth: A review of research and implications for policy. *Social Science Review, 75*(2), 271–291; Hay, D. (1996). Childhood sexual abuse: Implications for the

development of intimate relationships in adolescence and adulthood. In B. Galaway & J. Hudson (Eds.), *Youth in transition: Perspectives on research and policy* (pp. 252–261). Toronto: Thompson Educational Publishing.

9. Casey Family Programs (2001). *It's my life: A framework for youth transitioning from foster care to successful adulthood.* Seattle, WA: Casey Family Programs.

10. Van Bockern, S., Brendtro, L., & Brokenleg, M. (2000). Reclaiming our youth. In R. A. Villa & J. S. Thousand (Eds.), *Restructuring for caring and effective education: Piecing the puzzle together* (pp. 57–76). Baltimore, MD: Brookes Publishing Co.

11. Rutman et al. (2005); Casey Family Programs. (2001).

12. Casey Family Programs. (2003).

13. Kufeldt, K. (2003). Graduates of guardianship care: Outcomes in early adulthood. In K. Kufeldt & B. McKenzie (Eds.), *Child welfare: Connecting research, policy, and practice* (pp. 203–216). Waterloo, ON: Wilfred Laurier University Press.

14. See, for example, Wotherspoon, T. (2004). *The sociology of education in Canada: Critical perspectives* (2nd ed.). Oxford: Oxford University Press.

15. Tweddle. (2005); Chapin Hall. (2005a). *Midwest evaluation of the adult functioning of former foster youth: Outcomes at age 19.* Chicago: Author.

16. Casey Family Programs. (2003).

17. See, for example, Knott, T., & Barber, J. (2005). *Do placement stability and parental visiting lead to better outcomes for children in foster care?* Toronto, ON: Centre of Excellence for Child Welfare; Chapin Hall. (2005b). *Behavior problems and educational disruptions among children in out-of-home care in Chicago.* Chicago: Author.

18. Chapin Hall. (2005b).

19. National Youth in Care Network. (2005).

20. Casey Family Programs. (2001).

21. Anglin, J. P. (2003). *Pain, normality and the struggle for congruence: Reinterpreting residential care for children and youth.* New York: Haworth Press; Anglin, J. (2003). Staffed group homes for youth: Toward a framework for understanding. In K. Kufeldt & B. McKenzie (Eds.), *Child welfare: Connecting research, policy, and practice* (pp. 191–201). Waterloo, ON: Wilfred Laurier University Press.

22. Van Bockern et al. (2000).

23. More information about the Casey Family Programs can be found at www.casey.org. This Web site also contains a wealth of research on youth and the foster care system, along with other relevant child welfare topics.

24. Casey Family Programs. (2001).

25. Casey Family Programs. (2001).

26. Casey Family Programs. (2001).

27. Casey Family Programs. (2001).

28. Casey Family Programs. (2001).

29. Goddard, J. (2003). Children leaving care in the United Kingdom: "Corporate parenting" and social exclusion. *Journal of Societal and Social Policy, 2/3,* 21–34.

30. Goddard. (2003).

31. Goddard. (2003); United Kingdom House of Commons. (2000). Children Leaving Care Bill.

32. Goddard. (2003); United Kingdom House of Commons. (2000). Children Leaving Care Bill.

33. Goddard. (2003); United Kingdom House of Commons. (2000). Children Leaving Care Bill.
34. Mendes & Moslehuddin. (2004).
35. Mendes & Moslehuddin. (2004).
36. The United Kingdom Department of Health Web site contains information for parents interested in adoption: www.direct.gov.uk/Parents/AdoptionAndFostering/AdoptionAndFosteringArticles/fs/en?CONTENT_ID=100 21345&chk=Oe%2BKyt.
37. Mendes & Moslehuddin. (2004).
38. Gilbertson, R., Richardson, D., & Barber, J. (2005). The Special Youth Career Program: An innovative program for at-risk adolescents in foster care. *Child and Youth Care Forum, 34*(1), 75–89.
39. Gilbertson et al. (2005).
40. Gilbertson et al. (2005).
41. Mendes & Moslehuddin. (2004).

CARRIE REID *is with the Centre of Excellence for Child Welfare and the Child Welfare League of Canada in Ottawa, Canada.*

Experience living independently while still in care can play a key role in developing self-sufficiency skills for foster youth. Can a comprehensive housing program in Ohio be replicated in other communities?

3

The role of housing in the transition process of youth and young adults: A twenty-year perspective

Mark J. Kroner

IN 1981, LIGHTHOUSE YOUTH SERVICES, a private nonprofit agency in Cincinnati, Ohio, began one of the first independent living programs for adolescents in the state. The local county children's services supervisors and Lighthouse administrators had been hearing numerous stories of youth who had left the county's foster and group homes and were discharged from county custody, only to return several months later stating that they were homeless. The youth were reporting that they had learned a lot from various placements, but their families remained dysfunctional and were still unable to provide a stable place for them to live.

Lighthouse started a small pilot project for youth from the agency's boys' group home who were seventeen years old and unable to return to live with their families: they would be moved to individual apartments, while remaining in county custody. These apartments were rented from private landlords and could be located in any part of the community. The agency furnished the apartments with used furniture and supplies, gave each youth a small weekly allowance for food and transportation, and assigned a group home social worker to check on the youth and call him regularly.

Many in the county thought this was an unwise venture, fraught with liability issues, adolescent chaos, and regular news of negative events. This chapter describes the agency's experiences, twenty years and thousands of youth later. I joined Lighthouse in 1982 and became director of the independent living program (ILP) in 1986, inheriting a box of files, a porch full of old couches, and about ten youth in various states of immaturity. Today the program averages around sixty-five youth and fifteen of their children a day and has served as a model program for communities around the United States. Over fourteen hundred youth have come through the program. The ILP coined a phrase early on, "independent living without housing is like driver's training without a car." The agency learned that unless youth get experience living on their own, even the best life skills training programs will not have a full impact. (Exhibit 3.1 provides definitions of independent living arrangements.)

Program description

The ILP accepts youth ages sixteen to nineteen, male and female, as well as pregnant or parenting teens, in county or state custody. These youth were temporarily or permanently removed from their biological or adoptive families due to chronic abuse or neglect and usually could not return to live with their families. Most youth are discharged from the program before reaching age nineteen. Most participants are placed in individual apartments intentionally because we believe this is the best way to help them develop survival skills in a short period of time. We accept that this will be an experience full of risk and mistakes. Youth are usually not ready for this experience.

Clients can be placed anywhere in the county where they are near a bus line. We look for places a youth can afford when they

Exhibit 3.1. Definitions of common independent living arrangement options

Institutions: A large structured facility or group of facility housing anywhere from forty to several hundred youth, with most services provided on-grounds.

Residential treatment centers: A facility or group of facilities usually serving between fifteen and forty youth and using a combination of on-grounds and community-based services.

Community-based group home: A house in the community of six to twelve youth that uses existing community services but provides some treatment by around-the-clock trained staff.

Supervised apartments: A cluster or complex of apartments occupied by a group of youth preparing for independent living, usually with a staff person living in one of the units or using a unit as an office. Twenty-four-hour coverage is often provided.

Specialized family foster homes: A youth is placed with a community family licensed to provide care and sometimes specifically trained to provide independent living services.

Shelters: A facility that provides short-term emergency housing to teens in crisis.

Live-in roommates: A youth shares an apartment with an adult or student who serves as a mentor or role model. The apartment can be rented or owned by the adult or the agency.

Host homes: A youth rents a room in a family or single adult's home, sharing basic facilities and agreeing to basic rules while being largely responsible for his or her own life.

Boarding home: A facility that provides individual rooms for youth or young adults, often with shared facilities and minimal supervisory expectations.

Shared house: A minimally supervised house shared by several young adults who take full responsibility for the house and personal affairs.

Semisupervised apartments: A privately owned apartment rented by an agency or youth in which a youth functions independently with financial support, training, and some monitoring. Also known as scattered-site apartments.

Single-room occupancy: A room for rent, often near a city center.

Specialized group homes: Sometimes also referred to as semi-independent living programs, these homes are usually staffed as a group home but house older teens and focus on developing self-sufficiency skills.

Subsidized housing: Government-supported low-income housing.

are out of the system. We try to place youth in areas with which they are familiar. Clients can keep their apartments, furniture, supplies, and security deposits if they are employed at termination and have proven to the landlord that they are responsible. Clients who do not have a stable source of income at termination are assisted in finding other living arrangements, often through some type of low-income, subsidized housing organization.

Services offered

This section looks at elements of a comprehensive transition process.

Housing

The ILP rents apartments from private landlords in the county in neighborhoods that are affordable and close to the client's school, job, and social supports. The program also operates two shared homes, one for males and one for females, that have four beds and a live-in resident manager and two supervised apartments with a resident manager occupying one of the apartment units. The program pays the security deposit and provides necessary furnishings, other supplies, and a telephone. If the client does well and has a job at termination, he or she can keep the apartment and all of the furnishings and take over the lease.

Financial support

The ILP provides a weekly allowance of fifty-five dollars, ten dollars of which is saved in an agency aftercare account for the young person. The forty-five dollars is to cover food, laundry, and personal items. The agency also covers utility, telephone, and rent payments until the last few months in the program, when the client takes over paying bills if possible. The ILP assists clients with work clothing, minor school fees, and miscellaneous expenses. Most clients are expected to work a part-time job and purchase any items beyond basic necessities.

Life skills training

The ILP has created a twelve-project life skills curriculum that the youth completes at his or her own pace. The agency has developed the curriculum over the past ten years, gathering useful materials from around the nation and adding information that program participants appear to need. The topics are an assessment of current level of functioning, money management, time management and planning ahead, use of community resources, apartment management, nutrition and food preparation, use of public transportation, social skills, employment skills and finding and holding a job, problem solving and decision making, self-care, and building a support network.

Emotional support and guidance

Each youth is assigned to a social worker with a caseload of eight to twelve youth. Other program staff members assist with client problems as they arise. Clients are usually contacted several times each week, including regular telephone contact, and vulnerable or new clients are asked to call in daily. The program staff members maintain pagers, voice mail, and an on-call system. Clients should be able to reach a staff member within five to fifteen minutes at any time.

Case management

ILP staff members connect clients with educational, vocational, therapeutic, medical, dental, and other needed resources. Everyone works toward the goal of maximum potential client self-sufficiency given the time available and the developmental capabilities of the youth.

Crisis management

The ILP staff provide twenty-four-hour crisis management, which can involve hospital runs, resolving client-tenant problems, apartment maintenance issues, or confronting client friends or family who are causing problems at the apartment, among others. This time-consuming activity is an expected part of the process of learning responsible behavior.

Outreach

The ILP staff conduct self-sufficiency and independent living training throughout the year for eligible clients. The program has created numerous workbooks and training materials specifically designed for local youth. The program is also involved in a year-round training program designed to teach foster parents, group home youth workers, and other care providers how to teach self-sufficiency skills to youth in their early teens.

Measuring Program Success

The ILP is community based (often keeping the youth in her or his original neighborhood) and strength based, recognizing the resiliency of the youth and his or her previous history of overcoming obstacles. The program believes that teens, like most other people, learn only when they have to and learn best by doing. The program also believes that teens coming from extremely dysfunctional families need intensive attention and support to counteract years of abuse, neglect, and distorted thought processes.

Youth in the ILP exit the system in a fully furnished apartment or subsidized housing situation. The outcomes the program strives to achieve are driven by the basic survival needs of the youth. The ability of the youth to function without ongoing dependence on the adult system is the ultimate measure of the program's success. The final analysis of success is determined by the youth and referring agency and must take into consideration the youth's developmental potential, the behavior of the youth prior to placement in the ILP, and the time the program has had to work with the client.

Here is a case example that demonstrates how the county system typically works to transition youth to life on their own. Regina (named changed due to confidentiality) is a seventeen–year-old youth who ran away from home at age sixteen after years of being sexually abused by her stepfather. The county placed her in a Lighthouse group home for four months and then referred her to its independent living program. While at the group home, Regina completed a thirteen-part self-sufficiency program offered by the county and Lighthouse. She lives in an apartment three blocks from her school and works part time at a department store. She meets weekly with her program social worker at her apartment to review her progress. Regina does her own shopping, cooking, and cleaning and manages her transportation needs. Her social worker is helping her learn to budget her money so that when she is discharged from the system three months after she graduates, she will be able to keep her apartment and all her furnishings and take over all of her own bills. With full-time work, she has a chance of being able to afford her apartment for some time.

The program has worked closely with the county juvenile court and children services personnel to develop policies and procedures that work for the youth, program, services system, and the community. The program currently averages a daily population of over sixty-five youth a day and their children. Many former clients return to train younger teens or speak to care providers about what helped them become self-sufficient.

A unique feature of the Lighthouse ILP is its ability to move youth along a continuum of living arrangement options depending on their behavior and level of functioning. Youth who are evicted from an apartment might spend a week in the agency's crisis shelter before receiving a second chance in another apartment. They might live for a while at a boarding home in downtown Cincinnati before moving into an apartment or at one of the program's shared homes. The program rarely terminates a client, knowing that mistakes are powerful learning opportunities.

Youth with developmental disabilities might spend several months in the program's supervised shared home before moving into their own apartments. They can be returned to a group home or foster home and contract to work their way back into their own apartment if their original behaviors prove that they were not ready for the freedom.

The Lighthouse ILP is now a permanent part of the county's continuum of care. The county recognizes that some youth do not have families or relatives willing or able to provide enough long-term stable emotional or financial support. It actively seeks feedback from members of the community on how it can improve services.

The program has basic rules and policies to guide all youth, but there is a lot of flexibility in expectations depending on the overall situation. Clients need permission to have overnight visitors and are allowed no more than two visitors at a time. No one is allowed in a youth's apartment when the youth is not there, and alcohol or drug use is not tolerated. The program does its best to give clients chances to learn from mistakes but will terminate them for involvement in illegal activities or continuous rules infractions.

The program has these desired outcomes:

- Experience in living independently. Youth currently stay an average of ten and a half months.
- Knowledge of budgeting and money management issues, learned from experience.
- Knowledge of basic life skills information.
- Increased sense of personal responsibility.
- Connections to caring adults.
- A vision of a possible positive future. Youth are given not only information to help them see their future but also a possible place to stay.
- Connections to adult community resources.
- Time to grow up and opportunities to "fail safely."
- Affordable housing at discharge.
- A chance to keep all furnishings.
- No need to move again at discharge.
- A chance to adjust to a neighborhood.

Case Examples

The following case examples show how Lighthouse developed living arrangement options that provide different levels of supervision, geographical flexibility, and second chances for youth who cannot handle their first chance on their own. It takes a system to make this work; child welfare, juvenile court, and most often nonprofit care providers need to see the importance of giving youth a chance to get experience before discharge for this to work. The child welfare system's primary goal of protecting children and youth is challenged as the new goal, a process of supportive letting go, takes precedence.

Trevor, age seventeen, is a chronic runaway who cannot live with other peers. He ran from two group homes and three foster homes but always kept his job at a surfing supplies store in his town. His school attendance was sporadic, but he showed a lot of potential. He was referred to an ILP, which placed him in an apartment rented from a private landlord. He did well on his own for several months, but soon complaints came from the landlord about parties, heavy metal music at 2:00 A.M., and lots of people coming and going. After several warnings, the ILP staff came to his apartment, helped him bag up his possessions, and took him to a house run by the ILP with three beds for males and a live-in resident manager. Trevor was not happy but agreed that he had lost control of his apartment. He stayed at the shared home for three months and earned his way back to another scattered-site apartment.

Cathy, age seventeen, lived in a foster home with four other foster siblings in a small town thirty miles from the city. She was doing well in all areas of her life, but her caseworker knew she could not move back with her family and needed to learn to live on her own. A referral was made to an ILP in the city, which quickly established that there were no apartments for rent in Cathy's town. After numerous calls, the ILP found a couple in their thirties with an extra room in their house who knew Cathy from their church. The children's service ran a background check on the couple, checked out their house, and approved of the placement. Cathy completed her senior year while living in this host home, and after graduation from high school and discharge from care, she worked out an agreement to stay living with the host family, paying them $150 toward room and board, until the end of the summer, when she would move into a college dorm.

Bobby, age seventeen and a half, lived in a group home successfully. He was referred to an ILP and placed in his own apartment. He did well for a while, but once school started, numerous friends found out that he lived in his own place, and it became party central. In spite of many conversations between Bobby and ILP staff, the place remained out of control. Bobby was removed from the apartment and placed in the agency's shelter for two weeks. He then was allowed to return to the apartment with a written behavioral contract. The second time around, things went more smoothly.

Susan, age seventeen, was referred to an ILP after doing well in a foster home for over three years. She was placed in a supervised apartment with three units for youth and one for a resident manager. Susan did well in the program and after four months moved into an apartment rented from a private landlord. Three months later, her foster sister moved in with her, after clearing this with the landlord. When Susan leaves the system, she and her new roommate will be able to split the rent and utility bills and will take over the lease.

Assumptions underlying the scattered-site apartment program model

The following points outline the reasoning behind Lighthouse's model of choice:

- Youth learn best by doing, feeling directly the consequences of their actions (within reason, of course).
- Youth learn best when they have to. No classes or training can have the impact of a month of living alone in an apartment, feeling

the responsibility for time management, apartment management, shopping, food preparation, and other life activities.
- An organization does not have to purchase and maintain a piece of property. Clients can be accepted immediately if apartments can be located with landlords willing to rent to teens.
- The clients can choose a location that is convenient for them and close to work, school, and their social support network.
- The clients can keep the apartment, the furnishings, and the security deposit and leave the system with a fully furnished living arrangement with long-term possibilities.
- The size of the program is not limited to the number of agency-owned apartment units.
- Group and crowd control problems are not the primary issue. Most problems reported by supervised apartment programs are interactive problems between residents. In a sense, they are like group homes with less supervision.
- In an independent apartment, a youth is challenged to develop an internal locus of control—to realize that his or her actions must be self-generated and not due to the presence of a caregiver or enforcer.
- The transition to self-reliant living will be smoother if the living arrangement resembles the future situation of the youth. The jump from a program with an abundance of resources, staff, and other people to life alone can be unsettling and confusing.
- The youth must develop coping skills to deal with loneliness and control of visitors and assertive skills to deal with fellow tenants, landlords, and other social situations that he or she is protected from in a supervised setting.
- The scattered-site model is an ideal public-private partnership, with community landlords receiving a large portion of the program's budget and available housing being used fully. It makes the best use of what is already there.
- For many of the young adults who enter the system or are otherwise without a true home, their central issue is having some control over their lives. Giving them personal space is perhaps the most significant form of empowerment.

Supervising youth in less restrictive transitional living arrangements

All youth leave the child welfare system, whether they are ready or not. Many communities are developing program strategies in which youth can get some experience living independently while still in custody.

When a youth leaves his or her place of residence and is out in the community, it does not matter whether he or she lives in a foster or group home, residential treatment center, or scattered-site apartment. A youth who is looking for trouble will find it. From our experience, most of our agency youth assault, runaway, destruction of property, and theft charges happen while they are at home or living in supervised settings. In other words, even with sixty to eighty youth living on their own, we do not experience any more or fewer problems than occur in any placement setting.

Of course, this does not mean that youth in individual scattered-site apartment or semisupervised group living situations need no attention. Here is a summary of what I learned about supervising youth in ILPs:

- Live-in staff. Some programs have apartments with live-in adult roommates or small shared homes with a live-in resident manager who is in and out of the residence at various times. Sometimes there is no supervision, but the adult is present at night and various times during the week and weekend. With random visits by day staff, this situation can work for semiresponsible youth.
- Daily visits by staff. This is hard to provide due to caseload size and budget limitations, but some high-risk youth do well with this level of supervision.
- Unannounced visits. This strategy is sometimes effective when youth are breaking program rules or there are reports of illegal or unusual activities. Youth need to be informed that this is a possibility at all times but is usually used only when problems are being reported.
- Weekly visits. This is the typical scattered-site method of keeping an eye on a youth living alone. Along with regular telephone contact, phone texting, and even e-mails, youth and adults can feel at ease.

- Youth come to the ILP office. This can be a daily expectation for new or unproductive youth or can happen several times a week. Some youth show up daily even when they are not required to do so.
- Former foster parent monitoring. Our program has contacted with former foster parents who are leaving a foster home in a rural area. This builds on an existing positive relationship and cuts down on ILP staff travel time and expenses.
- An in-town person with social services experience for monitoring. We have contracted with a local person for youth who leave a placement situation in a distant community but are connected to school and work and want to remain in that area.
- Regular telephone contact. If a youth is struggling with behavioral or medical problems, this is a good way to keep on top of the situation. Asking the youth to call the office daily to report activities is sometimes an expectation for new clients.
- Weekly visits by volunteers, mentors, and student interns. Often programs have support staff who do home visits, one-on-one life skills training, or in-home counseling. These visits can take the place of or enhance paid staff visits.
- Electronic monitoring bracelets with an early curfew. Our program requires this for high-risk youth who enter the program with felony offenses. Youth can have them removed after meeting the terms of a behavioral contract, usually after four to six weeks.

Risk management for less supervised living arrangements

Liability issues are always raised when agencies start considering using semisupervised living arrangements such as scattered-site apartments for independent living preparation. The first law of youth work often applies: every helpful action is met with an immediate inappropriate reaction. Probably most agency executives who have been involved in using individual apartments would say that they have found this model to be no more or less risky than any other child welfare living arrangement. From my experience, group homes and residential treatment centers are where most of the property damage, assaults, thefts, and runaways occur. Nevertheless, programs need to do whatever possible to keep from incurring liability and the wrath of an angry landlord.

Here are some basic things that need to be in place:

- Effective screening. Agencies must know as much as possible about a youth before placing him or her in an apartment. At times, referring agencies leave out (inadvertently or not) key details, such as sex offenses, previous property damage, or fire-setting behavior. Some high-risk youth might need increased supervision or need to prove themselves in a more supervised setting before moving into their own place.
- Documentation. Keeping track of all face-to-face unannounced visits and telephone contacts can eliminate any charges of neglect.
- Clear policies. A detailed policy and rules manual is needed that clearly lays out expectations. In addition, the youth signs a form stating that he or she has read the policies, understands them, and agrees to follow them. Discovering that a new female client has set up a day care center for all of her new relatives in her new apartment might seem outrageous, but this might be an expectation coming from her family.
- Court-supported signed agreements. This acknowledges that the court system has approved a living arrangement .
- Clear emergency procedures and around-the-clock on-call. ILPs using individual apartments need to have people assigned (usually on a rotating basis) to be on call for after-hours emergencies. Many of the calls received after hours can be dealt with over the telephone. Many youth will create a pseudo crisis during their first month in an apartment just to see if there really is anyone out there.
- Liability insurance. Each agency has to decide the level of comfort with the risk it is taking. Some programs insure each apartment. Others have been able to include any apartment in their overall umbrella policy.
- Backup living arrangements. Having an out-of-control youth living in an apartment rented from a landlord who calls daily ask-

ing for the youth to be removed is one of the biggest headaches of an ILP staffer. Having a shelter, respite foster home, spot in a group home, or some other temporary placement can immediately cool down a hot situation and help the youth understand the limits of what other people will tolerate.

- Quick confrontation of problems. Agency personnel who think someone else has moved into the apartment, hear about drug deals going on, or get calls about the "pit bulls for sale" sign in a client's window must deal with these situations immediately. Waiting for problems to go away can lead to much bigger problems.
- Mandatory counseling if necessary. Youth with a previous history of suicide attempts, serious mental illness, alcohol or chemical dependency, and similar other problems should contract to continue with therapy or support groups as a condition of remaining in a less supervised setting.
- Contracts. Short-term behavioral contracts can help a youth understand the consequences of his or her current behavior, including discharge from the program or return to a more supervised setting.
- Daily contact with high-risk youth. Programs should plan on some youth occasionally needing more attention. Youth who get depressed, sick, traumatized, injured, or lose someone important should have daily face-to-face or telephone contacts, not necessarily with the same ILP staff.

Changing the child welfare system to benefit youth

This section looks at the strategies used for moving from a protection stance to a supportive letting-go process for youth in transition.

State Level

At the state level, providers had to be given a chance to prove that new living arrangement models could work. Only after several years of trial and error on the part of several nonprofit pioneers were the Ohio State codes changed to allow less supervised settings liked scattered sites to be considered a legitimate part of the child welfare system. The state brought in professionals at every level to develop the new codes and took the leap of faith necessary to make licensing reflect the needs of youth for more real-life experience and less protection. Eventually the state had to let go of the idea of preapproving every apartment site and instead licensed agencies to provide IL services and self-monitor the youth. From the Lighthouse point of view, this has worked well, with local children's services staff and nonprofit care providers working together to assess safety issues.

County level

At the county level, independent living and children's services caseworkers had to learn to allow youth to make mistakes and learn from hundreds of poor decisions. Just like any parent, staff had to learn how not to be helpful and let natural consequences provide feedback to youth on their own for the first time. For example, we had many arguments about whether a youth who spent his food allowance on new shoes should be given more money for food or allowed to go hungry for a few days. These discussions still take place, but there is now much more system cohesiveness about these issues. The local children's services system also had to reconfigure its budget and accounting processes to pay for placement options other than foster homes, group homes, and residential treatment centers. It took years to work out the details. Juvenile court personnel had to let go of many controls and disciplinary procedures in order to sanction individual apartment placements. It did not make sense to put someone on house arrest who was two months from being discharged from the system and needed to be looking for a job.

Agency level

At the agency level, the Lighthouse board of trustees had to assume new liability, new on-call systems, backup living arrangements for those who were out of control, and means of moving youth around the area. Independent living staff had to convince private landlords to try renting to a youth not known to independent living and had to work out lease agreements that worked for all. The agency had to work out agreements with its shelter program and group homes for youth who needed to be stepped back in placement and had to convince referring agencies that moving unsuccessful youth to a new site for a second chance could lead to better outcomes.

Program level

At the program level, staff had to develop a program without the benefit of much field literature, research, or other providers' experiences. They had to get used to continuous criticism from everybody about what youth needed. Independent living staff had to let go of having one set of rules for everyone and had to define success differently for each youth.

Lessons learned in the past twenty years

The transition process rarely goes as planned. Emotions of youth run high when they are getting cut off from system support and realizing painful family realities plus the fact that the welfare system that supported their parents no longer exists. There is no adult system ready to take over where the youth system left off.

Many foster youth do not show much maturity when they are eighteen but often do several years later (similar to their live-at-home cohorts). Few of our clients are ready for this experience. We put them out on their own because they do not have the time to grow up as youth from normal families do. We force them to deal with practical adult issues in an unrealistically short period of time. Age eighteen is no longer the normal age at which youth are able move out from normal families of origin.

Many youth kicked out of ILP have returned later in good shape, and the opposite situation occurs as well. We should expect that our youth will go through many ups and downs for years after they leave us. Even youth who leave as planned will probably need help in the future, just as youth from normal families do. Our county's aftercare system is better than most others in the country but is not realistically funded. Former ILP participants will need financial support in the future, even if it is just one-time rent help.

No one living arrangement works for all youth. The system needs to have multiple options: small, supervised group settings; individual apartments; host homes; access to emergency short-term shelters; relative placements; boarding homes; and other arrangements. No one knows how a particular youth will do when first on his or her own. Second chances in a different location can work out.

Some youth do better alone than in groups. They might not be very productive, but they will have fewer fights and runaways. Youth who have never lived in a group setting might be threatened by sharing a place with numerous other people with similar problems. Youth with attachment disorders more often than not are unable to adjust to even a small group living situation.

Many of the youth in the system will need adult support for the rest of their lives. They will never have the emotional stability, intelligence, or common sense needed to function in our complicated world without someone around to explain things and help clean up their messes. If communities do not connect them to another support system, they will often end up getting connected in jails, emergency rooms, and psychiatric units, and this is not cheaper for a community.

When youth leave the child welfare system on negative terms, they usually don't leave the community they live in. They are still here and still need a place to stay and supports.

Our county's year-round self-sufficiency training program makes a difference for independent living youth. The youth who complete this thirteen-part training know what to expect if they eventually move into their own apartment, and it gets their care providers thinking more about their clients' futures too.

We are able to use low-income housing for youth who are getting ready to live on their own but cannot afford their current apartments. However, waiting lists continue to lengthen, and housing people want to see juvenile court records and proof of a job.

We are not having enough success with males in general. They should be kept in care longer than females, who tend to mature earlier.

Our goal is to slowly have youth take over all responsibilities. Teaching staff how "not to be helpful" is important. Enabling leads to more dependence on the system.

Advice for those courageous enough to make changes to help youth

The advice that follows reflects years of experience with supporting youth in transition and is intended as a guide for practice.

Preparing youth for independent living

We have devised this list of fifty ways to help youth get ready for independent living:

1. Help them get an original copy of their birth certificate.
2. Help them get a social security card (and a wallet to put it in).
3. Enroll them in a school program in which they can succeed.
4. Help them get a picture identification card.
5. Find out if they are eligible for a Medicaid card.
6. Help them get copies of medical records.
7. Start a "life book" that will contain important papers, pictures of family, and other mementos.
8. Help them open up a bank account.
9. Teach them how to write and cash a check.
10. Line them up with a dentist whom they can continue to use.
11. Line them up with a doctor whom can use when they are on their own.
12. Help them put together a family scrapbook.
13. Help them renew contact with family members.
14. Help them develop at least one friendship.
15. Line them up with a good counselor.

16. Take them to join a local recreation center.
17. Teach them some new ways to have fun.
18. Connect them with a church group.
19. Help them find a better-paying job.
20. Make sure they really understand birth control.
21. Show them the best places to shop for food, clothing, and furniture.
22. Help them learn how to look up resources in the telephone book.
23. Help them work through an independent living skills workbook.
24. Teach them how to read a map.
25. Take them on a tour of the city.
26. Teach them how to use the bus system and read bus schedules.
27. Buy them an alarm clock, and teach them how to use it.
28. Show them how to use the library and get a library card.
29. Help them get a driver's license and price insurance.
30. Role-play contacts with police, bank tellers, doctors, and others.
31. Role-play several different styles of job interviews.
32. Help them put together a résumé and an application fact sheet.
33. Make a list of important telephone numbers.
34. Teach them how to cook five good meals.
35. Teach them how to store food.
36. Teach them how to use coupons and comparison-shop.
37. Teach them how to read a paycheck stub.
38. Teach them how to use an oven and microwave.
39. Teach them how to thoroughly clean a kitchen and bathroom.
40. Take them to a session of adult court: traffic and criminal.
41. Tell them how to get a lawyer and when to get one.
42. Help them understand a lease or rental agreement.
43. Teach them how to do their taxes.
44. Teach them how to write a letter and mail it.
45. Help them develop good telephone communication skills.
46. Go over tenant and landlord rights.
47. Help them find a safe, inexpensive place to live.
48. Teach them how to budget their money.
49. Help them find and get along with a potential roommate.
50. Talk to them often about feelings about going out on their own.

Learning independent living skills the hard way

Independent skills do not always come easily.

- Some learn money management by going without food for a few days after spending their money on nonessential purchases.
- Some learn time management after they are evicted from their apartment due to nonpayment of rent caused by lack of income due to being fired for being late at work too many times.
- Some learn to clean their apartment after they see roaches everywhere.
- Some learn personal hygiene after figuring out that nobody will go out with them.
- Some learn to control their anger after spending a month in jail due to excessive fighting.
- Some learn to eat well when they realize they cannot fit into their clothing and cannot afford to buy more.
- Some stop drinking after losing their driver's license and having to take the bus to work.
- Some stop using drugs when they find out they cannot get a job unless they can pass a drug screen.
- Some learn to control their friends at their apartment after losing their third deposit due to being evicted because of too much partying.
- Some learn to pay their rent on time after finding all of their possessions sitting on the curb in front of their apartment.
- Some learn the importance of an education when they always get beaten out for a promotion or better job by people who have degrees and more training.
- Some never learn.

Developing independent living housing options

There are a variety of independent housing options:

- Try to find a place the youth can keep after discharge from care.
- Try to find a place that the youth can afford (with a roommate, subsidy, savings, or something else).

- Try to find a place in an area comfortable or familiar to the youth.
- Keep safety and security issues in mind.
- Find places with access to transportation, employment, shopping, and other services.
- Try to give the youth at least six months' experience in a living arrangement prior to discharge. Expect lots of mistakes, problems, and dumb choices.
- Have backup plans in place for youth who cannot handle the less supervised settings.
- Understand that youth might need to be moved around several times before they learn what it takes to be a responsible tenant.
- If your agency can't create alternative living arrangements, contract with someone who already has them in place or is willing to give it a try.
- Try to create a program that is flexible, responsive to clients' needs, and cost-effective.
- Educate (continuously) key systems people about the importance of experience and the need to have affordable housing lined up at discharge.
- Understand that developing a full continuum of living arrangements takes years.
- Hire staff who are experienced, tolerant, creative problem solvers, and have a rich sense of humor.
- Understand that liability issues are no more or less an issue than in any type of child welfare placement, but be sufficiently insured anyway.

Housing cost considerations

The following costs need to be addressed when considering housing options:

- Zoning
- Licensing requirements and limitations
- Time until start-up
- Insurance
- Required building safety upgrades

THE ROLE OF HOUSING IN THE TRANSITION PROCESS   73

- Staff coverage requirements
- Neighborhood issues: residents uneasy about the possibility of this housing in their neighborhood, police awareness, safety issues, convenience
- School district issues
- Location preferred by clients
- Accessibility
- Affordability for the long term for the client
- Referral source choice
- Court support and choice
- Length of time the client can stay
- Potential for and consequences of being closed by the agency or community
- Client contribution
- Grants to support the property or do rehabilitation
- Donated property
- Staff backup for supervised apartments
- Vacations, sick days, and training days
- Site reputation
- Reusability of apartment by other clients

Recommended Reading

Barth, R. P. (1990). On their own: The experiences of youth after foster care. *Child and Adolescent Social Work, 7*(5), 419–440.

Bissing, Y. M., & Diament, J. (1997). Housing distress among high school students. *Social Work, 42*(1), 31–41.

Brinkman, A. S., Dey, S., & Cuthbert, P. (1991). A supervised independent-living orientation program for adolescents. *Child Welfare, 70*(1), 52–57.

Clark, H. B., & Davis, M. (2000). *Transition to adulthood: A resource guide for assisting people with emotional or behavioral difficulties.* Baltimore, MD: Brookes Publishing.

Cook, R. (1994). Are we helping foster care youth prepare for their future? *Children and Youth Services Review, 16*(3–4), 213–229.

Cook, R., Sedlak, A., Mech, E. V., & Rycraft, J. R. (1995). Preparing foster youths for adult living. In *Proceedings of an Invitational Research Conference. National Evaluation of Independent Living Programs.* Washington, DC: Child Welfare League of America.

Courtney, M. E., & Barth, R. P. (1996). Pathways of older adolescents out of foster care: Implications for independent living services. *Social Work, 41*(1), 75–83.

Davis, M., & Vander Stoep, A. (1997). The transition to adulthood for youth who have serious emotional disturbance: Developmental transition and young adult outcomes. *Journal of Mental Health Administration, 24*(4), 400–427.
English, D. J., Kouidou-Giles, S., & Plocke, M. (1994). Readiness for independence: A study of youth in foster care. *Children and Youth Services Review, 16*(3–4), 147–158.
Homelessness: Programs and the people they serve: Highlights report. Retrieved December 21, 1999, from http://www.huduser.org/publications/homeless/homelessness/highrpt.html.
Kroner, M. (1992). Independent living: Mapping out the territory. *Children's Voice, 2*(1), 16.
Kroner, M. J. (1988). Living arrangement options for young people preparing for independent living. *Child Welfare League of America, 67*(6), 547–561.
Kroner, M. J. (1999). *Housing options for independent living programs.* Atlanta, GA: CWLA Press
Kroner, M. J. (2001). *Moving in: Ten successful independent/transitional living programs.* Eugene, OR: Northwest Media.
Mallon, G. P. (1998). After care, then where? Outcomes of an independent living program. *Child Welfare, 71*(1), 61–78.
Mangine, S. J., Royse, D., Wiehe, V. R., & Nietzel, M. T. (1990). Homelessness among adults raised as foster children: A survey of drop-in center users. *Psychological Reports, 67,* 739–745.
McMillen, J. C. (1999). Better for it: How people benefit from adversity. *Social Work, 44*(5), 455–468.
McMillen, J. C., & Tucker, J. (1999). The status of older adolescents at exit from out-of-home care. *Child Welfare, 78*(3), 339–360.
Mech, E. V. (Ed.). (1988). *Independent-living services for at-risk adolescents.* Atlanta, GA: Child Welfare League of America.
Mech, E. V. (1994). Foster youths in transition: Research perspectives on preparation for independent living. *Child Welfare, 73,* 603–624.
Mech, E. V. (Ed.). (2003). *Uncertain futures: Foster youth in transition to adulthood.* Atlanta, GA: CWLA Press.
Mech, E. V., & Fung, C. C.-M. (1999). Placement restrictiveness and educational achievement among emancipated foster youth. *Research on Social Work Practice, 9*(2), 213–228.
Mech, E. V., Ludy-Dobson, C., & Hulseman, F. (1994). Life skills knowledge: A survey of foster adolescents in three placement settings. *Children and Youth Services Review, 16,* 181–200.
Nollan, K. A., Wolf, M., Ansell, D., Burns, J., Barr, L., Copeland, W., & Paddock, G. (2000). Ready or not: Assessing youths' preparedness for independent living. *Child Welfare, 70*(2), 159–176.
Osgood, D. W., Foster E. M., Flanagan, C., & Ruth, G. R. (Eds.). (2005). *On your own without a net: The transition to adulthood for vulnerable populations.* Chicago: University of Chicago Press.
Roman, N. P., & Wolfe, P. B. (1997, Winter). The relationship between foster care and homelessness. *Public Welfare,* 4–9.

Scannapieco, M., Schagrin, J., & Scannapieco, T. (1995). Independent living programs: Do they make a difference? *Child and Adolescent Social Work Journal*, *12*(5), 381–389.

Stone, H. D. (1987). *Ready set go: An agency guide to independent living.* Washington, DC: Child Welfare League of America.

Waldinger, G., & Furman, W. M. (1994). Two models of preparing foster youths for emancipation. *Children and Youth Services Review*, *16*(3–4), 201–212.

MARK J. KRONER *is director of the division of self-sufficiency services for Lighthouse Youth Services in Cincinnati and director of the independent living program for Lighthouse. He received the National Independent Living Association's Founder's Award in 2000.*

Youth without citizenship or permanent resident status who age out of care are vulnerable to exploitation and deportation. This chapter explores the dimensions of this issue and ways to address it.

4

Transition without status: The experience of youth leaving care without Canadian citizenship

Francis G. Hare

INVESTIGATIVE JOURNALISTS can sometimes serve as canaries in the mineshaft, leading the way for later academic investigations. Three illustrative cases, reported respectively in the *Los Angeles Times*, the *New York Times*, and the *Toronto Globe and Mail*, can serve as introductions to the issue of how children could end up alone and perhaps in care in a new country. Journalist Sonia Nazario won the Pulitzer Prize for feature writing in 2003 for a set of articles published in the *Los Angeles Times* in September and October 2002, entitled "Enrique's Journey." She has recently published an expanded version in book form based on her articles.[1] Nazario tells the story of an adolescent Honduran boy who traveled north through Mexico into the United States in search of his mother, who had left home a decade earlier to seek employment in the United States. In the source notes posted on the Pulitzer organization site,[2] Nazario documents her estimate "that at least 48,000 children enter the United States from Central America and Mexico each year, illegally and without either parent." The overwhelming majority of these children do not end up in the care of the child welfare system. In fact, the number designated as juvenile court dependent children taken into care for protection, as given in the U.S. Immigration and Naturalization Service/Homeland Security statistical yearbooks, tends to be around five hundred.[3]

A second journalistic investigation comes from Nina Bernstein in the *New York Times*.[4] She reported on the situation of youth without legal status in the child protection system in New York City who were approaching the point of aging out of care. She emphasized that concerns since the terrorist attacks of September 11, 2001, have resulted in "a crackdown to protect national security [which] collides with a long tradition of protecting juveniles." For these youth in care, their attempts to obtain legal status are impeded by the fact that potential national security concerns take precedence. A conspiracy theorist might assume that even though a youth is only twelve years old now, he may have been sent by hostile parties to act as part of a terrorist plot that will be hatched a decade down the road. In short, security trumps the rights of the child.

The third example of a journalist's attempt to bring these issues to public attention was an article that described the situation of a youth who had been adopted, with his sister, from an orphanage in Mexico by a woman in Toronto.[5] The problem for the youth was that the woman apparently wanted to adopt only a girl and grudgingly agreed to take her brother as well. Within three years of returning to Toronto, the woman had placed the boy in the care of the Catholic Children's Aid Society. While in care, he did not obtain Canadian status and on aging out of care, his various brushes with the legal system have made him subject to deportation from the country in which he has spent almost his entire life.

Review of the literature

In the academic and agency literature in this field, the terms *unaccompanied minor* and *separated child* tend to be used interchangeably by researchers, although there is an emerging preference for the latter phrase, which emphasizes the child's experience of loss and disconnection. The definition offered by the United Nations High Commission for Refugees (UNHCR) is someone under the age of eighteen "who is separated from both parents and is not being cared for by an adult who by law or custom is responsible to do so."[6]

The relevant literature on this issue is sparse. A recent and relatively comprehensive publication on the current state of research, policy, and practice in the Canadian child welfare system refers to the need for cultural competency, the diversity of the Canadian population, and the risks and challenges of transition from care, but does not address the issue of the immigration status of children and youth in care.[7] There is also a summary report of a roundtable discussion involving the Child Welfare League of Canada and the UNHCR that expresses concern over the lack of reliable data on the problem and that the few data that are collected are not generally available.[8] There is nothing that compares to the *U.S. Homeland Security Immigration Statistics Yearbook* that would indicate how many children who lack Canadian legal status enter the country and are placed in care by the court for protection against maltreatment.

A review of documents relevant to unaccompanied and separated children seeking refugee status in Ontario notes that "the knowledge base on the experience of unaccompanied children and of those who are trying to meet their needs, on institutional strategies and practices and their impact is very small indeed."[9] The authors point out that the numbers of such children are not reliably known, although the number of refugee claims made by unaccompanied minors in Ontario between January 1999 and September 2002 was more than two thousand. This does not include those who did not formally make such claims and does not indicate how many of these were in the care of child welfare authorities. These authors also review the challenges facing such children with regard to accommodations, education, and health and suggest that "detailed studies of their lives would make an important contribution to advocacy on their behalf."[10]

Kilbride, Anisef, Baichman-Anisef, and Khattar have provided an extensive review of the issues newcomer youth face, making brief reference to the additional settlement problems faced by those who come as convention refugees (those whose claims for refugee status are seen as well founded and based on criteria listed in the 1951 Geneva convention). One must assume these problems would be compounded if the youth were unaccompanied.[11] These authors' report could thus be seen as providing a comparison group of youth who share many of the same challenges but are not in the care of the child welfare system.

Sadoway has reviewed a number of legal and jurisdictional issues and compared practices in the three principal immigrant-receiving Canadian provinces of Quebec, Ontario, and British Columbia. She noted the limited mandate of Children's Aid Societies in Ontario and the procedures involved in attempting to provide care and support, as well as recent developments in jurisprudence with regard to refugee status for child claimants. She points out that each of the provinces and territories of Canada has individually ratified the UN Convention on the Rights of the Child but that there are "serious inconsistencies and gaps with regard to the protection and care of refugee children in the different provinces of Canada and the problems are most severe in Ontario where the majority of separated refugee children are to be found."[12] To round out this brief review, the reports written by Ayotte for the UNHCR and an article on the stresses inherent in being a child refugee should be noted.[13,14]

Transition as the point of peak vulnerability

The youth who are the focus of attention in projects examined here were taken into care for their own protection as mandated by provincial legislation. Prior to coming into care, they were vulnerable because they had arrived alone at a Canadian port of entry, with someone who was not deemed to be an appropriate guardian, or with family but identified as being at risk of abuse or neglect prior to the family's obtaining Canadian status on their behalf. What is common in these three situations is that entering into care served to reduce their vulnerability, giving them a form of protective status that would last until their transition from care. This status, although not permanent, at least enabled them to accomplish educational, personal, and social development goals and to receive health care and various other forms of support and assistance. The impermanent nature of this status becomes clear only when the youth makes the transition from care. If the work has not been done while the youth is in care to ensure that he or she leaves care with at least the status of a permanent resident or, ideally, full citizenship, then the youth cannot work legally, can pursue higher education only by paying international student fees, does not have ready access to the health care system, and is subject at any time to deportation.

Many youth do leave care in these circumstances, making the point of their transition to independence fraught with maximum anxiety and uncertainty. The focus of this project is on why such a situation would come to exist, how many youth find themselves in this situation, and what can be done to rectify matters.

Interviews with child welfare personnel

Interviews were conducted with four staff at the Pape Adolescent Resource Centre (PARC) in Toronto. This agency is funded by the local child welfare agencies to assist youth in transition from care with education, housing, employment, and health issues, all of which require Canadian status for optimal benefit. PARC staff were generally willing to share their experience and observations in interviews that ranged from twenty to forty-five minutes. The following quotations from PARC staff illustrate their perspective on the situation of youth in care without status:

"We ask about their legal status in Canada, and surprisingly, sometimes I have youth who aren't even sure."
"So youth come to me, and it's always a question: 'What's your status, where were you born? If you don't have status yet, have you applied?' and universally the answer is, 'My worker is taking care

of it.' So the next step for me is to ask the worker if they are taking care of it. Some workers respond well to that, and some don't."

"So when [child welfare workers] have immigration paperwork... added on to the normal day-to-day work with their caseloads, I can see how it could be hard for them to keep track of."

"I think most of the workers have not been touched by immigration. The whole issue of immigration and status is not as urgent for somebody who has not had an immigration experience."

PARC staff believe that as many as 20 percent of the youth they serve may have immigration issues that increase their vulnerability. They believe that youth may not be fully aware of the implications of a lack of status. Many youth simply assume that their child welfare worker is taking care of things when this may not in fact be the case given worker turnover and other demands on their time. The youth may not even discover their vulnerability until after they leave care and attempt to continue their education, obtain legal aid, apply for a job, cross a border to attend a concert or sports event, visit a physician, apply for a loan, or any of a dozen other routine activities that most people would take for granted. The relative security they had while in care is quite shattered.

Discussions were also held with other individuals affiliated with the child welfare system in Ontario. Several respondents reported that they have received legal advice suggesting they are unable to apply for permanent resident or for citizenship status on behalf of youth in care and that the youth must apply on his or her own behalf after turning eighteen. They also reported that there is no systematic centralized record keeping that would facilitate easy identification of youth lacking status. Finally, they expressed a strong desire to have people with specialized knowledge of immigration issues working in or available through child welfare agencies who could take the lead in ensuring that youth do not leave care without Canadian citizenship or permanent resident status.

It became apparent in these interviews that the normative situation reported in the literature does not hold for most youth in care without status in Toronto. The most common way for a child to find himself or herself in care without citizenship or permanent resident status, according to the majority of the available literature, is to arrive alone at a port of entry and be taken into care by child welfare authorities. Perhaps because the catchment area for the child welfare agencies in Toronto does not include a port of entry, staff report that the vast majority of youth in care without status arrived with families and were taken into care for protection prior to obtaining Canadian permanent resident or citizenship status. In some cases, this means that the birth and national origin documents that youth need to obtain citizenship are held by families or relatives who are either themselves unavailable or unwilling to make this material available to the youth. This can only heighten the vulnerability of these youth at their point of transition from care if they are then seeking to obtain status on their own behalf.

Interviews with youth

In spite of prominently displayed posters and word-of-mouth recruitment, only two youth were willing to be interviewed. Reasons for this reluctance and ways to strengthen the voice of youth in this area will need to be explored. Youth who lack status may be reluctant to do anything that could draw attention to them and thus increase their vulnerability as they leave care. This is consistent with the general theme of this project, which is that maximum vulnerability for the youth occurs at the point of transition from the safe but impermanent status of being in care to being on their own but without legal status in Canada. A recent event in Toronto in which a political activist was arrested and subsequently deported while she was on a university campus would certainly have the potential to raise questions about any promises of anonymity and confidentiality that a researcher might offer. There is no way to determine the extent to which any particular factor influenced the reluctance of youth to take part in the interviews, but the issue should be addressed.

The youth who did agree to participate offered unique insight into their experiences. They presented in considerable detail the fears, frustrations, and often the lack of information that they live with on a daily basis. The importance of support and opportunities for empowerment was a significant theme. A sample of quotations follows:

"My worker explained it to me that I couldn't apply for status because the government was already giving you money while I was in care."

"The risks of not getting status would be that you could be with the wrong crowd, wrong place, wrong time, and something happens, and they look you up on the computer and say whatever, and they can just ship you back. Especially like being a person of color, it's like you try to stay indoors rather than go outdoors because you just never know."

"I got pregnant with my son before I got my papers, and I was scared that, oh my God, my son is a citizen, and I'm not. He could stay, and I could go."

"If you don't have your papers, you can't go to school. How could you pay fees like an international student?"

"If somebody says, 'What do you want to do?' you can't answer. You don't know if you are going to stay here. You don't know if they are going to deport you. You don't have any future."

"People stereotype you for different things. It's not only because you are black. If you are young guys, you get stereotyped by the cops. It can be a dangerous situation."

"Sometimes you need emotional help. You need someone beside you know who you can trust."

"They may say tomorrow morning, 'Take your stuff and leave the country.'"

Similar to agency staff, the youth believe that they can obtain status only by applying on their own after turning age eighteen. The section that follows suggests that although this is widely believed, it is not true. The youth are also acutely aware of their compounded vulnerability in that they have been dependent on the state but that source of support is about to vanish, they are without legal status in the country, and if they are from racial minority groups, they feel stereotyped and observed with suspicion. The possibility always exists that even a false accusation of illegal activity could bring them to the attention of authorities and lead to their deportation from the country in which they were raised.

Interviews with others

Fortuitous circumstances, not initially foreseen in the project, led to an interview with the former Canadian federal minister of immigration, Elinor Caplan. She suggested that the belief on the part of child welfare authorities, staff, and youth that the youth must apply for Canadian status himself or herself on turning age eighteen is neither warranted nor in the best interests of the child if legal guardianship rests with the child welfare authorities. In other words, the child welfare system has the authority, as legal guardian, to apply for status for the child while the child is still in care. At least in Ontario, this tends not to be done.

A review of agency literature in other jurisdictions in Canada led to interviews with two staff from SARIMM (Service d'aide aux réfugiés et aux immigrants du Montréal Métropolitain), an agency in Quebec with the mandate to provides both social and legal support to immigrant and refugee youth. Illustrative quotations from one SARIMM respondent follow:

"We have the legal mandate to be in contact with every unaccompanied minor that comes into Quebec. The definition for unaccompanied minor is someone under eighteen who has come into Quebec without a parent or legal guardian. The border will call us immediately."

"When a person comes to see us, they're automatically assigned a designated representative and a social worker, who cannot be the same person."

"The designated representative helps the youth to organize their information in preparation for the hearing at the Refugee Board and to represent them, obtain whatever documents are needed, and help with any follow-up."

"The role of the social worker is the whole piece on integration, counseling, mediation. They are not surrogate parents, but they make sure they are attending school, encouraging them to do volunteer work, get part-time jobs. They do get really involved, making sure the kids are safe because these are kids that are really at risk."

In addition to providing legal and social support to youth, SARIMM staff act as an expert resource for other organizations serving youth, offering consultations, advocacy, and staff training to frontline workers. This service model appears to be quite similar to what the Ontario staff were seeking when they spoke of the need for people with specialized expertise who would be capable of conducting staff training sessions.

Further research will be required to determine the extent of association between SARIMM and the child protection and children's mental health system in Quebec. SARIMM representatives explained that they do not have a child protection mandate but that they are available to facilitate the settlement and integration of immigrants and refugees, with a particular obligation to assist unaccompanied minors. Although they are not directly involved with the transition of youth from care, the SARIMM model does represent a resource that could facilitate this transition if it were emulated in Ontario. The SARIMM respondent also indicated that the agency remains available as a resource for youth over the age of eighteen who wish to use their services.

Some preliminary implications

The project has highlighted the vulnerability of a small but significant group of youth in transition from the child welfare system who are most vulnerable right at the point where they make the transition from care. The system must increase its efforts to systematically track these youth while they are in care and exercise its authority to ensure that they have obtained Canadian permanent resident or citizenship status prior to leaving care. This means that the awareness of the issue and its significance must be raised within the system. A specialized group of experts and advocates, as illustrated by SARIMM in Quebec, should be available to work with and train frontline staff on issues related to immigration. University-based researchers who work with vulnerable and at-risk individuals who may be subject to deportation must be able to confidently and convincingly offer the promise of anonymity and confidentiality without the fear that the information they gather would somehow end up facilitating the deportation of the respondent.

Future directions

One extension, currently underway, is to replicate the interview process in Ontario child welfare catchment areas that have ports of entry. The two closest to Toronto are the Peel region, where the Toronto Pearson International Airport is located, and the Niagara region, where there are Niagara River border crossings. This would increase the likelihood that youth in care without Canadian citizenship or permanent resident status would have arrived alone and been taken directly into care.

Another extension being planned is to look more closely at the situations in the other principal receiving provinces of Quebec and British Columbia, examining provincial variation in the legal and social support components of obtaining status for youth in the child welfare system. We already know that Quebec has a well-tested service, training, and advocacy model with SARIMM, and it may be beneficial to set up a workshop where people from across the country could share useful practices. Looking beyond Canada, it would be interesting to expand the investigation into other jurisdictions, including the United States.

It will also be important to collaborate with advocacy groups such as the National Youth in Care Network. Finally, it would be important to explore ways to ensure that youth in care without Canadian permanent resident or citizenship status have the opportunity to explain their concerns and obtain the assistance and support they deserve, consistent with Articles 12, 20, and 22 of the UN

Convention on the Rights of the Child, which has been accepted by both federal and provincial levels of the Canadian government.[15]

Notes

1. Nazario, S. (2006). *Enrique's journey*. New York: Random House
2. Pulitzer Board. (2003). Enrique's journey—Notes about sources: Chapter One. Retrieved April 21, 2006, from http://www.pulitzer.org/year/2003/feature-writing/works/notes1.html
3. For example, see U.S. Department of Homeland Security. (2003). *Yearbook of immigration statistics, 2002*. Washington, DC: U.S. Government Printing Office.
4. Bernstein, N. (2004, March 28). Children alone and scared, fighting deportation. *New York Times*, pp. YT 1, 24.
5. Philp, M. (2003, July 15). A one-way ticket out of the only nation he knows. *Toronto Globe and Mail*, pp. A1, A3
6. United Nations High Commission for Refugees. (1994). *Refugee children: Guidelines for protection and care*. Geneva: United Nations High Commission for Refugees. P. 21.
7. Kufeldt, K., & McKenzie, B. (Eds.). (2003). *Child welfare: Connecting research, policy and practice*. Waterloo, ON: Wilfrid Laurier University Press.
8. Child Welfare League of Canada, International Social Service Canada, and United Nations High Commissioner for Refugees. (2001). *National Roundtable on Separated Children Seeking Asylum in Canada: Summary report*. Ottawa: Author.
9. Ali, M. A., Taraban, S., & Gill, J. K. (2002, November). *Unaccompanied/separated children seeking refugee status in Ontario*. Ottawa: Citizenship and Immigration Canada. P. iv.
10. Ali et al. (2002). P. 46
11. Kilbride, K. M., Anisef, P., Baichman-Anisef, E., & Khattar, R. (2003). *Between two worlds: The experiences and concerns of immigrant youth in Ontario*. Toronto: Joint Centre of Excellence for Research on Immigration and Settlement.
12. Sadoway, G. (2001). Canada's treatment of separated refugee children. *European Journal of Migration and Law, 3*, 347–381. P. 380.
13. Ayotte, W. (2001). *Separated children seeking asylum in Canada*. Ottawa: United Nations High Commission for Refugees.
14. Fantino, A. M., & Colak, A. (2001). Refugee children in Canada: Searching for identity. *Child Welfare, 80*, 587–596.
15. In December 1991, the Canadian federal government ratified the UN Convention on the Rights of the Child, which was adopted by the UN General Assembly in November 1989.

FRANCIS G. HARE *is professor in the School of Child and Youth Care bachelor degree program and in the Immigration and Settlement Studies master's program at Ryerson University in Toronto, Canada.*

After a brief outline of the contextual organization of youth protection offered in Quebec, the author presents an intervention program that aims to prepare youth in high-risk categories for employment, independent living, and an overall orientation to the development of an autonomous lifestyle.

5

Promoting autonomous functioning among youth in care: A program evaluation

Martin Goyette

OVER THE PAST FEW years, considerable research has highlighted the challenges posed by the need for social reinsertion of youth who leave placement. For youth who leave an alternative living environment at the outset of adulthood, this integration is made all the more difficult by psychosocial and health factors and a lack of support in preparing for independent living and employment. Although they may possess various qualifications and resources, many find themselves relying on publicly funded services or social assistance as they enter adulthood. This chapter examines an intervention program that aims to prepare youth in high-risk categories

This chapter was written with support from the Institute of Health Services and Policy Research, Canadian Institutes of Health Research, and the National Crime Prevention Strategy of the government of Canada, with the collaboration of the Ministry of Public Security, Quebec.

for employment, independent living and autonomous functioning more generally. It also presents preliminary results of a three-year pilot study and offers an outline for the provision of intervention and support to troubled youth who are entering adulthood.

Context and overview of the problem

In Quebec, the Association des centres jeunesse du Québec (ACJQ) is made up of seventeen youth centers and two multiple vocational centers whose mission is to supply psychosocial services and rehabilitation services for troubled youth, mothers in distress, and their families. Services mandated to provide community-based rehabilitation and youth protection through foster home placement or readaptation centers fall under the youth center's jurisdiction. The primary mandate of these centers is to apply the Youth Protection Act, the Youth Criminal Justice Act, and the Health and Social Services Act. Each year, nine thousand social workers in the seventeen youth centers in Quebec supply services to 100,000 troubled children, teens, and their families under the auspices of this legislation. Close to 27,000 youngsters are removed from their natural families—thus, the term *substitute* (or *alternative*) *living environment*. Principally, they are placed in foster homes, but also may be integrated into residential centers or group homes.[1] The youngsters who constitute the clientele of these youth centers are particularly vulnerable to social problems, as well as crime and victimization. They are also at risk of encountering core difficulties in the process of social reinsertion.

The subjects' individual characteristics, such as their school and placement history, widen rather than narrow the gap where employment is concerned. In Quebec, studies on youth who have recently applied for social assistance demonstrate that a significant number were placed in foster care during childhood,[2] as was confirmed by the evaluation of the Solidarité Jeunesse program.[3] Often the youth interviewed for the study examined in this chapter mentioned that when they reached adulthood, they requested social aid because they saw no other alternative.[4]

From this perspective, a team of U.S. researchers confirmed that foster youth who reached adulthood while in a foster care environment and effectively made the transition to independent living nonetheless had higher rates of arrests and incarceration, were less schooled, experienced more marital instability, and had higher divorce rates.[5] Foster youth who are in transition to independent living are also more prone to homelessness,[6] have a higher rate of physical and mental health problems, are more likely to abuse drugs, and are more often unemployed.[7] These findings are consistent with the work of Baker, Olson, and Mincer in the United States[8] and the Ontario study conducted by Martin and Palmer[9] on the difficulties foster youth experience in the community after they have made the transition from foster care.[10]

In Quebec, Cloutier's report underlines the needs of youth leaving care.[11] The authors recommend "putting in action a practical training process that aims to teach independent living . . . to every youth aged 16 years or over placed for a medium-to-long term period . . . in order to help them to achieve a successful transition to adulthood." In August 2004, the Conseil permanent de la jeuness[12] made several significant recommendations in relation to youth in care. Their report proposed the integration of preparation for instrumental independence into daily activities for youth, experimentation with new interventions that prepare youth for autonomous functioning in a more general sense, continuing research on this issue, the maintenance of support of youth who leave foster care environments as young adults, and the development of mixed housing measures to facilitate residential resettlement of young people leaving youth centers.

Considerable research exists that points out that youth rarely have adequate preparation to live independently.[13] It is a well known fact that youth placed in foster homes generally experience integration difficulties, and few organizations in either Quebec or the rest of Canada have risen to the challenge by implementing sustained interventions that target social reinsertion. It is difficult to obtain a clear picture of what services for independent living preparation exist in Canada because of the significant regional disparities among organizations that provide these services and because youth protection falls under provincial jurisdiction.

Over the past decade, little research has focused on Quebec programs.[14] One recent study generated a portrait of practices aimed at preparing Quebec's foster youth for independent living while helping them with employment issues.[15] What is remarkable is that in spite of an awareness of the importance of offering these specialized services to youth who leave foster homes, few broadly structured programs exist to assist them in preparing for and sustaining this transition. Most of the time, the interventions take only employment into account, much to the detriment of promoting autonomous functioning overall.

This article describes an approach to youth leaving care that was inspired by the view that social reinsertion should have the promotion of an overall transition to adult functioning as its central focus. In this way, social reinsertion encompasses not only independent living and employment, but also the development of a career plan and the creation of a new adult family structure. Based on this theoretical perspective, an intensive project was designed to prepare qualified youth for the transition from foster care to autonomous functioning: the Projet d'intervention en vue de préparer le passage à la vie autonome et d'assurer la qualification des jeunes des centre jeunesse (Projet Qualification des jeunes, PQJ).

Qualification des jeunes project

The PQJ is an initiative of l'Association des centres jeunesse du Québec.[16] It is based on action research methodology, which strives to develop new strategies for social and professional integration for sixteen to eighteen year olds who are currently receiving service from youth centers. The project has targeted four Quebec regions: Abitibi-Temiscamingue, Laval, Outaouais, and Montreal (Batshaw).[17]

The project team comprises one coordinator and eight youth workers or educators, as they are called in Quebec (two for each participating region. Each team provides service to ten youths. The educators hired for the project worked on a full-time basis and had daily contact with the young people, thus adding resources to existing ones. This relatively high staff-client ratio is intended to facilitate richer personal and social development than can usually be accomplished through the regular activities offered in youth centers. The coordinator directs the project under the supervision of a counselor from l'Association des centres jeunesse du Québec in collaboration with the four people in charge from each region.

The project interventions are based on two major goals: preparation for independent living and the creation of a career plan that involves adequate training and preparation. An intervention plan is elaborated with each youth. Each young person may benefit from the addition of complementary supports from different service providers. Depending on the age of the candidate at the time of selection for the program, follow-up can continue to age nineteen. Thus, it is possible for program staff to provide a continuing presence during the youth's transitional period to adulthood. Because of this continuity, the youth are better able to gauge and face certain responsibilities that they might otherwise have underestimated before they were actually on their own. The project is characterized by intensive interventions: each educator ensures follow-up for his or her group of ten youths. The ten-to-one ratio is uncommon, with the current average staff ratio in Quebec youth centers being twenty-four to one.

The clients

The project serves eighty participants from the four regions in Quebec. The youth recruited had to be sixteen years old at the time of registration. They were referred by staff at youth centers and then selected by the eight educators and the coordinator. The candidates had experienced lengthy displacements over the course of their lives, and there was little possibility of being reintegrated into their initial families. None had clear objectives in relation to school completion or any plans for job training once the foster care system stopped providing services to them. They exhibited signs of insecurity, low self-esteem, and weak social ties, and they demonstrated difficulty in delaying gratification, respecting rules, and setting limits for themselves. They were not optimistic that this new program would be able to help them.

Objectives of the intervention

The project is designed is to prevent marginalization of youth who use services offered by youth centers at the time they reach adulthood. This in turn is hoped to reduce the possibility of involvement in a criminal milieu. To this end, the project has three objectives:

1. To prepare youth for their transition to independent living and supporting them in the process
2. To ensure that 75 percent of the candidates are either integrated into the workforce or have completed a vocational program by the time they reach adulthood
3. To support the development of a support system for the youth in youth centers

Thus, this intervention project targets overall personal and social development, as well as employment and preparation for living on one's own.

Intervention process

An evaluation protocol was established to provide a detailed portrait of each youth to use as a guide in the program. Two evaluation tools were employed: an instrument that provided a descriptive picture of the youth and his or her family (the Portrait synthèse du jeune et de sa famille, in collaboration with Groupe de recherche sur les inadaptations de l'enfance) and the Ansell-Casey Life Skills Assessments (ACLSA).

The Portrait synthèse du jeune et de sa famille is used to evaluate the youth's psychosocial situation and produces a detailed history and description of the youth and his or her family. Throughout 2003 and the beginning of 2004, the educators completed this assessment with each the youth. After being provided with the overall results the educators met with the youth and those who participated in the data collection in order to present and interpret the results.

ACLSA is used twice each year with each participant and his or her worker, who is well versed in the details of the youth's daily life. This instrument evaluates the extent of the youth's abilities for making the transition from placement to independent living. It uses six criteria that demonstrate functional autonomy: daily tasks, community resources and housing, financial management, the capacity to take care of oneself, social relations, and school and work habits.[18] Completing the ACLSA online is one of the first steps in an intervention process. Once this is completed, a report on the results for each category is sent to the individual client's educator. The results outline the subject's strengths and opportunities for improvements in each area. After discussing the results, the youth and his educator establish objectives in each of the categories they choose to work on together. This phase of the intervention, titled "Life Skills Guidebook," identifies competencies to be developed in each of the six categories. The Life Skills Guidebook also contains information on different instructional modalities that can be used to teach the youth life skills and includes an outline of apprentice sessions that apply to each skill. The list of competencies to be worked on is associated with performance indicators that can be used to show a youth's progress. Finally, the guidebook proposes activities for the youth themselves to complete, either individually or in a group, to develop certain abilities. The Life Skills Guidebook was initially prepared by the Casey Foundation and has now been translated into French and adopted by the ACJQ.

The development of intervention strategies

Using the results obtained from the evaluation tools as a starting point, the youth and the PQJ educator complete an intervention plan that responds to the individual needs of each youth in terms of career planning and preparation for independent living. In this way, objectives and the means to attain them are defined as a function of each youth's personal situation. The skills and capacities needed for each youth to succeed are also considered. The plan allows the PQJ educator to refine strategies along the way. The educator accompanies the youth through each step, both to assess progress and gather information that may be required. In addition, the educators participate in planning meetings with organizations that could provide services to the program participant once he is back in his community, such as schools, employers, employment resources, and community organizations.

The moment that regular services have been terminated for the youth at the youth center, the PQJ educator works with the youth to develop his or her abilities for independence in the areas of schooling, employment, living arrangements, community resources, financial management, and self-management with regard to health and daily issues. The PQJ educator can draw on any local programs that address training and integration in these areas and forge partnerships to better service the young person.[19] Part of the task of the PQJ educator is to develop community partnerships that help meet the goals for each youth.

Over the past year, PQJ educators have had the opportunity to offer more services to youth center educators as well as to foster youth from each youth center.

Lessons from the PQJ evaluation

An evaluation of the PQJ has resulted in a preliminary report that makes recommendations for conditions that are considered essential for successful program implementation in Quebec. These recommendations relate to regular youth services.[20] Table 5.1 groups principal data along with samplings.

All youth who participated in research interviews and filled out questionnaires did so voluntarily. The data collected were cross-referenced to evaluate the impact of interventions throughout the youths' path to autonomous functioning. Statistical analysis was made possible through the use of the assessment tools, and the results have implications for the types of interventions that are needed to support youth transitions to independent living.

Social reinsertion and relationship issues

The interventions described rely on the dynamics of the relationships between the youth and their staff. The interventions are based on and deployed around relational spaces between the youth and

Table 5.1. Data sampling time line, measures, and number of youth assessed

	T1: March 2002	T2: September 2002	T3: March 2003	T4: September 2003	T5: March 2004	T6: September 2004	T7: March 2005
Interviews with the research team to monitor overall progress						61	31
Interviews with PQJ counselors						80	80
ACLSA (youth results)	37	19	38	35	21	34	21
Risk factors	80				80	80	80
Personal strengths	80					80	80

Note: Risk factors and personal strengths were evaluated by the educators using a standardized procedure developed for this study.

those who determine the trajectories of the PQJ youth. The dynamics of these relationships, coupled with staff decisions and the effect they have on the social functioning of the youth, can produce dependence or facilitate constructive interdependence, which is what is needed for autonomous adult functioning.[21] Furthermore, support can either promote autonomy or act as an obstacle to independent functioning.

The PQJ educator is the principal support figure for the youth, regardless of where the pilot project takes place. By the time that youth receive services from youth centers and once they leave the institution, the educator will have provided close to three-quarters of the total service provided to the youth, two to five times more support than has been provided by all other adults. The role of different adults may change at different points in the transition; for example, parents, when involved, tend to be more supportive with regard to housing and material concerns, but are far less involved in employment transitions and the establishment of a new adult family structure. The support provided by different adults is sometimes activated by particular events. If the majority of supportive adults do not intervene in transition toward a new family, we have demonstrated how pregnancy, for a young woman, can mobilize these support mechanisms. However, at the same time, the focus on the pregnancy will divert support from career planning, which may be detrimental in the long run. Still, the educator is always central to the intervention and has a role with the young person's larger network of social support.[22] The goal of intervention is therefore not to work with the youth in isolation, but to incorporate the resources and relationships at the youth's disposal while encouraging the development of healthy reciprocity rather than dependency.[23]

The study data reveal that as youths leave the center, they often express a desire for financial independence. Thus, they often place schooling issues aside, which actually hampers their progress toward autonomy in the long run. In fact, the number of individual objectives in this project relating to education constantly decreased between 2003 and 2005. This is linked to the new realities the youth experiences on reaching adulthood. One possibility to consider is whether providing adequate financial support for rent will help young people develop a career plan rather than just settle for a job. As for the issue of knowing which factors contribute to maintaining employment, it does not seem that salary or number of hours worked play a major role. Youth hold on to a job longer when they have found the job with the help of an educator or a third party from the network. Here, we hypothesize that improved networking between PQJ and the business establishment in offering support to both the youth and employer contribute to longer-term employment stability. Mentoring seems to be an essential element in these youth support systems.[24]

Nonetheless, by autumn 2004, it was possible to affirm that PQJ intervention significantly helped to construct an environment where youth can acquire knowledge and competencies, as well as work experience. Many participants who experienced successful integration due to the PQJ program are at the margins of the mainstream labor force. The question, then, is not to know whether the youth are employed or if they have avoided seeking social assistance. It is, rather, knowing how these work experiences provide young people with the identity of an employed worker. This involves the development of an understanding of the marketplace, the search for employment, and specific work skills and will have greater long-term benefits than simply securing a job. At the same time, a period of reliance on social assistance can sometimes help stop a downward spiral that might have propelled the youth toward homelessness or criminal involvement because of the absence of financial support. Youth who participated in the PQJ program were also more conscious of their rights as employees, and they knew about available support for finding employment. In this way, the PQJ's success in matters of employment goes beyond the issue of obtaining and maintaining a job, thus going beyond most programming for transitions to independent living.

It must be kept in mind that the intervention does not constitute an end in itself; rather, it is a means to action. It is not meant to result in final outcomes for youth, but rather to help them create their own path as autonomous adults. Analysis of quantitative data pointed to the importance of the PQJ's role in guiding youth in their trajectory toward an adult lifestyle, over and above an actual move to living on one's own or the securing of a job. Figure 5.1 shows that youth autonomy appears to have increased considerably over the course of the first five measurement periods. Furthermore, improvement was maintained at T6 and subsequently at the termination of services provided by the youth centers. Also, the upward trend seems to continue at T7.

Coupled with the results obtained while analyzing the personal attributes and identifying the risk factors for each youth participant, these findings demonstrate considerable improvement in candidate profiles over the course of time spent with PQJ. Thus, Figure 5.2 illustrates the decrease in the extent of risk factors and the increase in personal strengths over the first two time periods.

Intervention attributes

This intervention rests on establishing strong relationships between the youth and their educators, both because they stay involved on a long-term basis and will act as a major support in the transition process.

Figure 5.1. Evolution of youths' average standardized ACLSA scores obtained by interviewing youth and the caregiver between T1 and T7

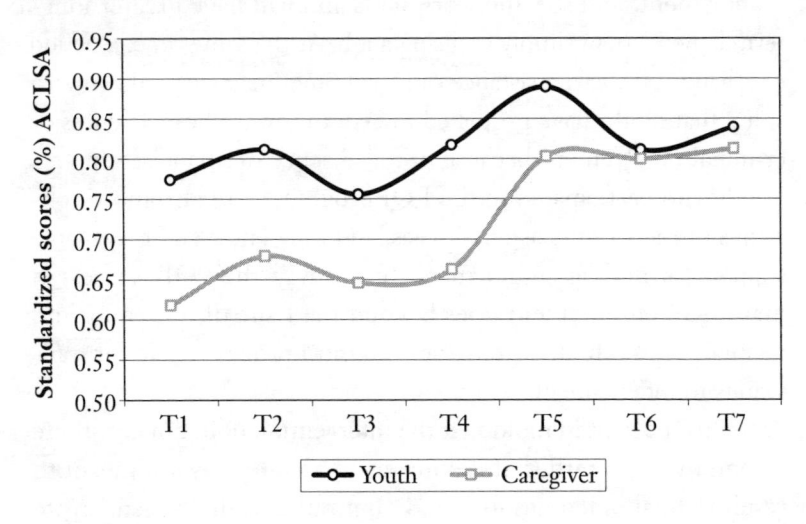

—○— Youth   —□— Caregiver

Figure 5.2. Average score evolutions for profile seriousness and personal attributes for periods T1 through T4

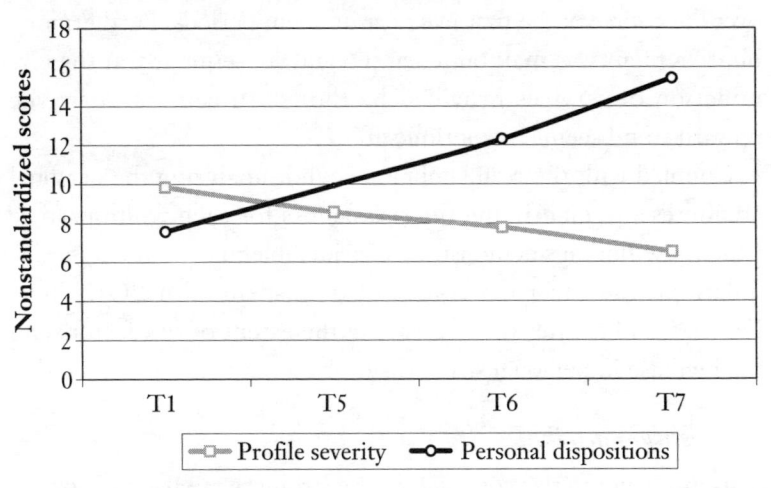

—□— Profile severity   —○— Personal dispositions

Note: Separate data for personal strengths at T5 do not exist. The line is established according to the mean results obtained for the other time periods.

This works against instabilities in the youth's life. The intensity, durability, and adaptability of the PQJ intervention do not, however, signify that it alone can replace all other involvements in the youth's life. The PQJ intervention process must also involve collaboration with professionals within or outside the youth centers. These results call for collaboration from an informal case management perspective that promotes intersectorial and interdisciplinary intervention as practitioners rely on the strengths and resources of youths and their networks.[25]

For youth to develop toward autonomy, programs must be created within a network of services and include interdisciplinary approaches. Programs must also work from a perspective of encouraging social experimentation and allow youth to put into practice the abilities and the knowledge they have gained through the program. This is possible only if the youth center provides some room for youth experimentation, with a full appreciation that the process leading to independent living is full of obstacles and setbacks.

Intervention paradigms need to be blended without subscribing exclusively to protection, rehabilitation, or risk management and without inhibiting the development of competencies through experimentation, which is essential in the transition to adulthood.[26] The youth recruited for the PQJ all appreciated their relationships with the program educators even though the program operated in a context where most of them were disassociated from their milieu. In this sense, the PQJ educator represents for the youth an external authority with a mandate for protection and rehabilitation, who is available, whom they can trust, and whom they can confide in with dignity and confidence. The PQJ educator is also closely connected to the youth center, thereby facilitating the youth's process toward autonomy.

In this framework, the PQJ implementation represents an interesting model, because the program functions, both internally (in the youth center) and externally (with and in the community at large), which is essential if there is to be a real impact on youths' integration. Thus, the project not only allows PQJ youth to pave their own way, but also allows youth centers to formulate an alternative intervention. PQJ offers opportunities for youth centers to engage in structured but broadly defined partnerships with community-based organizations.[27] At the same time, it allows youth to enter the community while allowing the community to be considered at the core of the youth center. One effect of the implementation of this program is that the whole foster youth population can see staff as a whole becoming more sensitive to the issues involved in matters of their preparation for independent living.

For the most part, the PQJ program achieved positive results. It stimulated changes in youth center practices and paradigms so that youth can move out into independent living through the development of attributes that contribute to autonomous functioning. This work clears a path for reflection that can mobilize youth centers and their partners, to eliminate structural conditions that serve as obstacles to social reinsertion.[28]

Conclusion

The results produced by PQJ have contributed to increased expertise regarding interventions for preparing foster youth for independent living and supporting their integration into adulthood. The ACJQ has recommended that the PQJ formula be gradually implemented in all Quebec youth centers. However, the PQJ will accept only five hundred youths into the program throughout the province of Quebec each year.[29] Those who receive long-term services from youth centers will still experience significant gaps in preparation in relation to the development of a career plan and an autonomous adult lifestyle.[30]

It is essential to offer more services to foster youth in general, so that the PQJ work can continue in the context of broader initiatives that focus on social development and a milieu approach.[31] The evaluation of the PQJ has identified some key requirements for intervention, especially in relation to intervention strategies and clinical tools. It is also necessary to tackle region inequities that exist in relation to access to transition services for foster youth, as these services can contribute to social integration, a reduction in criminal behaviors, and the elimination of victimization among youth.

Notes

1. Association des centres jeunesse du Québec. (2004). *Rapport d'activités 2003–2004*. Montréal: Author.
2. Ducharme, N., & Fonseca, F. (2002). La recherche-action Solidarité Jeunesse: l'amorce d'un modèle d'insertion sociale et professionnelle québécois. In D.-G. Tremblay & L. F. Dagenais (Eds.), *Ruptures, segmentations et mutations du marché du travail* (pp. 95–116). Sainte-Foy: Presses de l'Université du Québec; Lemieux, N., & Lanctôt, P. (1995). *Commencer sa vie adulte à l'aide sociale*. Québec: Ministère de la Sécurité du revenu.
3. Panet-Raymond, J., Bellot, C., & Goyette, M. (2003). *Le développement de pratiques partenariales favorisant l'insertion socioprofessionnelle des jeunes: l'évaluation du Projet Solidarité Jeunesse*. Montréal: Rapport présenté au Ministère de l'Emploi et de la Solidarité sociale et au Fonds québécois de la recherche sur la société et la culture.
4. Association des centres jeunesse du Québec. (2002). *Mémoire de l'Association des centres jeunesse du Québec à la Commission parlementaire des Affaires sociales sur le projet de loi 112 visant à lutter contre la pauvreté et l'exclusion sociale*. Montréal: Author.
5. Bussey, M., Feagans, L., Arnold, L., Wulczyn, F., Brunner, K., Nixon, R., et al. (2000). *Transition from foster care: A state-by-state data base overview*. Seattle, WA: Casey Family Programs.
6. Biehal, N., Clayden, J., Stein, M., & Wade, J. (1994). Leaving care in England: A research perspective. *Children and Youth Services Review, 16*(3/4), 231–254; Hahn, A. (1994). The use of assessment procedures in foster care to evaluate readiness for independent living. *Children and Youth Services Review, 16*(3/4), 171–179; Iglehart, A. P. (1995). Readiness for independence: Comparison of foster care, kinship care, and non-foster care adolescents. *Children and Youth Services Review, 17*(3), 417–432.
7. Bussey et al. (2000).
8. Baker, A.J.L., Olson, D., & Mincer, C. (2001). *The Way to Work: An independent living/aftercare program for high-risk youth. A 15-year longitudinal study*. Washington, DC: CWLA Press.
9. Martin, F. E., & Palmer, T. (1997). *Transitions to adulthood: A youth perspective*. Ottawa: Child Welfare League of Canada.
10. Bussey et al. (2000); Owen, L., Lunken, T., Davis, C., Cooper, B., Frederico, M., & Keating, T. (2000). *Pathways to interdependence and independence: The living care initiative. A study and good practice development project prepared for child protection and juvenile justice, the Department of Human Services Victoria*. Victoria: La Trobe University.
11. Groupe de travail sur la politique de placement en milieu familial (rapport Cloutier). (2000). *Familles d'accueil et intervention jeunesse*. Beauport: Centre jeunesse de Québec.
12. Conseil permanent de la jeunesse. (2004). *Les jeunes en centres jeunesse prennent la parole (Rapport de recherche)*. Québec: Author.
13. Mech, E. V. (1994). Foster youths in transition: Research perspectives on preparation for independent living. *Child Welfare, 73*(5), 603–623; Milne, C. (2002). Youth transition to independence. In Sparrow Lake Alliance. *Per-

manency planning in the child welfare system. Ottawa: Sparrow Lake Alliance, Children in Limbo Task Force.

14. Mann-Feder, V., & White, T. (1999). Investing in termination: Intervening with youth in the transition to independent living. *Journal of Child and Youth Care, 13*(1), 87–93; Nadeau, F. (2000). *Le passage à la vie autonome chez les jeunes ayant un vécu un placement en milieu substitut.* Sainte-Foy: Mémoire de maîtrise, Ecole de service social, Université Laval.

15. Goyette, M. (2006a). L'insertion socioprofessionnelle et la préparation à la vie autonome des jeunes pris en charge par l'État au Québec: Vers quelles interventions? Sociétés et jeunesses en difficulté. *Revue pluridisciplinaire de recherche.* Retrieved October 15, 2006, from http://sejed.revues.org/document159.html; Goyette, M. (2003). *Portrait des interventions visant la préparation à la vie autonome et l'insertion socioprofessionnelle pour les jeunes des centres jeunesse du Québec.* Montréal: Association des centres jeunesse du Québec.

16. This section describes elements of the following work. Morin, A. (2003). *Projet d'intervention intensive en vue de préparer le passage à la vie autonome et d'assurer la qualification des jeunes des centres jeunesse du Québec—Bilan de l'an 1.* Québec: Association des centres jeunesse du Québec; Morin, A. (2003). *Projet d'intervention intensive en vue de préparer le passage à la vie autonome et d'assurer la qualification des jeunes des centres jeunesse du Québec—Bilan de l'an 2.* Québec: Association des centres jeunesse du Québec; Goyette, M., Morin, A., & Lyrette, E. (2005). La préparation et l'insertion des jeunes des centres jeunesse: le projet Qualification des jeunes. *Revue PRISME, 45,* 218–231.

17. On the financial side, various ministries and Québécois organizations contributed: Ministry for the Health and the Social Services of Quebec, Funds of Fight Against Poverty by the Reintegration with Work, the Funds Youth Quebec as well as the centers' youth participants. The financial contribution of the National Center for the Prevention of Crime (a federal program of the Ministry for Justice) made it possible to improve follow-up with the young people, including extending the project from one year to four years, ending in November 2005.

18. Ansell, D. (2001). Where we are going tomorrow: Independent living research. In K. A. Nollan & A. C. Downs (Eds.), *Preparing youth for long-term success: Proceeding from the Casey Family Program National Independent Living Forum* (pp. 35–44). Washington, DC: CWLA Press; Nollan, K. A., Wolf, M., Ansell, D., Burns, J., Barr, L., Copeland, W., et al. (2000). Ready or not: Assessing youths' preparedness for independent living. *Child Welfare, 79*(2), 159–178.

19. Goyette, M., Panet-Raymond, J., & Dallaire, N. (2004). Algunos retos del Partenariado en Quebec; hacia la cualificacion de practicas de intervention social. *Revue Trabajo Social (Universidad nacional de Colombia), 6,* 129–144.

20. Goyette, M., Chénier, G., Noël, V., Poirier, C., Royer, M.-N., & Lyrette, E. (2006). *Comment faciliter le passage à la vie adulte des jeunes en centre jeunesse. Évaluation de l'intervention réalisée du projet d'intervention intensive en vue de préparer le passage à la vie autonome et d'assurer la qualification des jeunes des centres jeunesse du Québec: Rapport de recherche remis à l'Association des centres jeunesse du Québec et au Centre national de prévention du crime.* Montreal: ACJQ.

21. Goyette, M. (2006b). *Réseaux sociaux, soutiens et supports dans le passage à la vie adulte: Le cas de jeunes ayant connu un placement.* Unpublished doctoral dissertation, Université Laval.
22. Goyette. (2006b).
23. Goyette. (2006b).
24. Goyette. (2006b).
25. Goyette et al. (2004).
26. Goyette, M., & Turcotte, D. (2004). La transition vers la vie adulte des jeunes qui ont vécu un placement: un défi pour les organismes de protection de la jeunesse. *Revue Service Social,* 51(1), 29–44.
27. Dallaire, N., Goyette, M., & Panet-Raymond, J. (2003). *Les pratiques partenariales dans les Centres jeunesse de Montréal à l'aune des approches milieu.* Montréal: Rapport de recherche final. Institut de recherche pour le développement social des jeunes.
28. Goyette, M., Bellot, C., & Panet-Raymond, J. (2004). L'insertion socioprofessionnelle des jeunes en difficulté. Vers de nouvelles interventions?" In *Au-delà du système pénal. L'intégration sociale et professionnelle des groupes judiciarisés et marginalisés, sous la direction de Jean Poupart.* Sainte-Foy: PUQ.
29. Association des centres jeunesse du Québec. (2002).
30. Goyette & Turcotte. (2004); Pauzé, R., Toupin, J., Déry, M., Mercier, H., Joly, J., Cyr, M., et al. (2004). *Enfants, familles et parcours de services dans les centres jeunesse du Québec. Rapport de recherche de l'Université de Sherbrooke.* Sherbrooke, Quebec: Groupe de recherche sur les inadaptations sociales de l'enfance.
31. Goyette et al. (2006).

MARTIN GOYETTE *is a postdoctoral researcher at the Institut national de recherche scientifique-Urbanisation, culture et société in Montreal, Québec.*

This chapter discusses the authors' experience in working with young offenders who are leaving care in Ireland. Essential elements for effective programming are outlined.

6

Juvenile offenders and independent living: An Irish perspective on program development with St. Xavier's

Niall McElwee, Michael O'Connor, Susan McKenna

THE TRANSITION FROM CARE to independent living has become a recent focus in research given the poor outcomes that have been documented across many systems.[1] What type of planning is done with service users while they are in care? How can we design program plans that work in terms of preparation for independent living? It is difficult enough for young people to make a successful transition from their homes of origin to the outside world, but how much more onerous must it be if one has, to borrow a term from pulp crime novels, a "delinquent jacket" a couple of inches deep?[2]

St. Xavier's Home for Boys

In this chapter, we present a brief discussion around one agency that we all have had connections with over the past decade, and we will refer to it as St. Xavier's. The main aim of St. Xavier's is to deliver individualized programs of care, education, and reintegration that are in the best interests of the young people. It offers a comprehensive service, in small group living situations (a maximum of ten boys in each of three houses), for male juvenile offenders in a rural setting in Ireland. St. Xavier's accepts young men between the ages of twelve and sixteen years on admission, and all of the males are sentenced by the Irish Law Courts for a minimum period of two years. St. Xavier's attempts to provide service twenty-four hours a day, 365 days a year to all Irish courts. This is a big commitment.

More and more in Ireland, we see younger people involved in serious crime, and yet the Irish juvenile justice system quite rightly attempts to combine both welfare and justice ideologies in responding to the needs, rights, and characteristics of juvenile offenders. We should note that the Irish juvenile justice system has cherry-picked from systems in other jurisdictions in choosing to incorporate conferencing, restorative cautioning, and a range of community-based measures to be used as alternatives to custody.[3]

Aftercare and the transition to independent living

We might ask, What exactly is independent living? The three of us all have families from which we can receive emotional and, thankfully, financial support despite the fact that we left our homes of origins many years ago. This is not the case for many juvenile offenders locked up in secure care. For a significant percentage of youth, the term *independent living* is one that causes trepidation, unease, and confusion. But it should not be so, given the amount of discussion and, indeed, legislation, that has come into effect in recent years.

Of great significance for us in the continuum of the attempts at rehabilitative intervention is the final aspect of the program in many centers: aftercare. This is a term heard frequently but in practice is introduced with huge variance within, and between, centers. Some residential centers, for example, start planning for the transition from care as soon as a young man presents to them, while others wait until just a few months before termination of residency. We favor the former to the latter.

Aftercare, in an Irish context, may be understood as the formal provision of services until a youth reaches the age of twenty-one years.[4] The Irish Social Services Inspectorate neatly sums up by acknowledging, "Aftercare is the follow up and support provided in moving towards independence for all those young people who have been in care."[5] Section 45 of the Child Care Act 1991 sets out general powers that health boards have to support young people when leaving care. Although the statutory legislation does not place any specific duties on health boards, they are required, considering their ongoing responsibilities toward young people who were formerly in their care, to act in the manner of a "good parent."[6] Best practice dictates that parents, caregivers, and significant other people (as identified by the young people) are involved from the outset wherever possible; the welfare, interests, and rights of youth are paramount; and the young person will be actively involved in developing his care plans.

Supportive and consistent environment

While in residence in St. Xavier's Boys Home, the youth enjoy the benefit of a supportive and consistent environment and are physically safe. However, when they leave St. Xavier's, our experience is that they are quite vulnerable again. They no longer live in an environment where they are cosseted from temptation, crime, and, indeed, themselves. In an effort to address these vulnerabilities and prepare youth for an effective transition from residential care, St. Xavier's has devised an aftercare program for its cohorts—one that is well planned and begins at the first case conference after admission. If the young person has a viable home (based on social work and probation reports, and psychological or psychiatric assessments), preliminary work begins to return the youngster to his family.

If the home situation is not viable, and this is the case for a sizable minority of young people in St. Xavier's, an alternative must be explored. In any case, planning for the transition from secure care begins at the stage of entry. In this, the child and youth care key worker is crucial.

Key worker system at St. Xavier's

Initially, the assigned key worker invites the family to St. Xavier's Home and is open and forthright about the responsibilities placed on the family with respect to engaging in the rehabilitation of their son or sibling.[7] The aftercare/transition-from-care program commences with the key worker establishing a relationship with the family and gaining their trust and confidence. In most circumstances, the young man will be eligible to have a supervised, structured, purposeful trip outside St. Xavier's after three months. Depending on how he responds to these structured trips in terms of responsibility and the relationship and dynamics of the family being positive, a structured home leave program may be considered at the six-month case conference. This home leave program is designed to strengthen the relationship and build on the positive aspects of progress in other areas of the care program. Home leave begins with an initial visit for a short period (approximately one hour) in the company of the youngster's key worker. This may progress to a longer supervised visit home, ideally with a specific purpose, such as helping with gardening. Assuming that all goes well at this stage, the home leave progresses to an unsupervised home visit (the young person is dropped home and then picked up some hours later). These unsupervised home visits progress to overnight stays and eventually to weekends at home. Thus, there is a significant amount of work done around transition.

It is unusual for a young person to progress through these stages without incident. When a young person defaults in some way, he must revert to the previous stage of the home leave program and reestablish the trust. This may take some time. In essence, our experience is that it takes about twelve months before a young person is able to go home each weekend and return without incident.

During these weekends, home staff at St. Xavier's have found that young people are vulnerable. To address this vulnerability, the young person is expected to join a youth club or organization whereby he can be engaged in a positive use of his leisure time. Links with the local youth and community officer are established, and significant efforts are made for the young person to gain a sense of belonging. Also, efforts are made to link the young person into education or a training course or work in his local area. One of these needs to be in place before the subject of return to home can be addressed at the case conference. Again, the focus is around successful transition from the center to the community.

On reaching milestones

Once the young person has reached the stage whereby he has reached all of the milestones in St. Xavier's and is successfully engaged in his home leave program, he may be released on license to the care of his parents (or guardian). During this period, the key worker continues to visit weekly (sometimes unannounced) and offer support. On the expiration of the license period (usually coinciding with the expiration of the original sentence period), St. Xavier's legal responsibilities cease. However, the moral responsibilities ensure that support is offered for as long as the young person requires it.

Second safety: Loyola House

It is widely accepted that young people leaving care are at a greater risk of becoming involved in crime, drugs, or becoming homeless than those in the general population.[8] We know from experience how poorly equipped young people leaving care are to cope with life aftercare—practically, emotionally, and educationally—and consequently many experience loneliness, isolation, poor mental health, unemployment, poverty, and homelessness. There are a number of reasons that this is the case. Crucially, many young people do not receive adequate preparation for life after care, and what preparation they do receive is sometimes rushed, disjointed, and ad hoc. The expectation of an accelerated transition to adulthood, coupled with the fact that many of these children and young people have experienced familial abuse, rejection, disruption, and loss in their lives (not to mention a great deal of instability and disruption during their lives in care), means that they are unlikely to have developed core skills required to handle independence. Moreover, it is also the case that there is a lack of appropriate accommodation for care leavers, both supported accommodation and in the private rented sector. And finally, there are still huge gaps in the levels and types of support given to care leavers after they have moved on. For a young person where the home of origin (usually the family home) is not a viable objective to return to, the focus on aftercare and transition from care is on placement in Loyola House.

Loyola is a large house in the city center with six self-contained apartments. Each apartment is independent, with its own kitchen-living room, bathroom, and bedroom. Electricity is on a card meter, as is cable TV (that is, the service is paid for based on a meter reading of the extent of use). Two staff members are on duty at all times. Their role is to facilitate independent living skills (budgeting, cooking, and constructive use of leisure time, for example). Also, the staff are present to enforce the rules such as no drugs and no unapproved visitors. The staff are competent in assisting the young people to avail themselves of their social welfare entitlements and health service entitlements. Criteria for acceptance in Loyola House are quite simple. The young person must be in full-time education, in a training program, or in full-time employment in order to be accepted into Loyola. While in residence, if he loses his job or place in school or training, his placement in the house is in jeopardy. When this occurs, an alternative job or school is usually found; loss of placement for this reason is rare.

The day-to day routine in Loyola House is in many ways similar to life for thousands of Irish college students of similar ages, but with some subtle differences. For example, responsibility for their lives is given to the young people as far as is practical and possible. It is their responsibility to get themselves up, eat breakfast, and go to work or school each morning. They are not called or taken to work or school as was the case when they were in St. Xavier's. They are expected to attend the weekly residents' meeting, which has a formal component, such as keeping communal areas tidy and respecting others, and a social aspect, such as a communal meal, music session, or computer game competition. Here, infringements of rules are discussed. Also, there are individual sessions with the staff that are part of each young person's schedule. They must cook for themselves, launder their clothes, and budget their income.

Many young men who come to Loyola House have no viable family alternative to return to. Often the young person responds much more maturely in Loyola House than was the case while in St. Xavier's. This is due to diverse factors such as being given more responsibility and autonomy for their lives, not wishing to be incarcerated again, and, of course, the developmental maturation process (they are getting a little older and are viewing things from a slightly more mature perspective). This maturity can be significant in helping to rebuild the relationship and attachments with their significant parent or guardian. We find that the young person is often quite proud of his achievement of living independently and, because of this, is more willing to begin the process of rebuilding the family relationships from his independent state as if on equal terms.

At this time, the opportunity exists for highly valuable work to be undertaken with the family. Visits from the family are actively encouraged. Staff ensure that the family is aware of the tremendous effort that the young person has invested in making his life a success and encourage them to support the young person in his efforts. Of course, parents are welcome at any time, but staff attempt to schedule visits when there is time available to ensure that things go well and that there is some activity organized (such as a meal cooked by their child or just a walk in the park). It takes time to rebuild relationships, especially if one party has been very hurt. Both the young person and the family must realize this. However, family involvement is actively encouraged, as the ideal outcome for the majority of the young persons is the option of a return to his family home.

Youngsters are placed in Loyola House at about eighteen months into their two-year sentence in St. Xavier's. This allows roughly six months for each to settle in. Should the placement break down (and this will usually become evident in the early stages), the young person can be returned to St. Xavier's to complete his sentence. However, breakdown is extremely rare, and the placement continues, on a voluntary basis, after the expiration of the committal order. The program for each young person runs for approximately one and a half years and is in effect a tenancy sustainment program designed to give the young person the practical and emotional skills necessary to maintain his accommodation and manage his life with reduced supports.

The program includes individualized and structured support on topics such as personal development through relationships, self-esteem, practical and financial skills, education and training, employment, family and social relationships, and personal health and hygiene. Each young person will then move on, in a planned way, to private or social accommodation. For the few who experience difficulty in making a successful transition within the one-year time frame, staff in Loyola House continue to offer its service until a suitable alternative is identified.

Obviously the ultimate goal of the independent living program in Loyola House is for the young people to become self-sufficient and capable of living an independent life and reaching their potential. To this end, the Loyola staff work with the young person to find a more permanent accommodation in the private rented sector once he has completed the tenancy sustainment program. Once he has left Loyola House and is living in his private apartment, the outreach staff visit weekly for the first three months and then periodically as required.

Unfortunately, it may be two or three years after they have left St. Xavier's that the young men begin to fundamentally examine their lives. It is this maturation process that is so important in determining potential success. Because they will have been equipped with education, social skills, employment skills, and relationship-building skills, among others, they are more likely to make the more appropriate choices than might have been the case prior to their time at St. Xavier's and Loyola's. Thus, transition is less difficult than it might have been.

Conclusion

The Irish Social Services Inspectorate acknowledges that "the ultimate challenge for any health board or other provider of children's residential services, that wishes the care system to be effective, has to be to ensure that young people leave care in better circumstances than they arrived."[9] This is much easier said than done. Termination is not just an ending; it is a critical, distinct phase of any treatment process if it is handled effectively.[10] A major weakness in Irish legislation is that the principle and practice of reintegration is not at the forefront despite the need for such practice being acknowledged. The notion of reintegrative confinement has been mooted where a phased-out transitional process that begins in custody and moves outward to the community would be useful.[11]

The term *leaving care* does not differentiate between young people leaving as the culmination of a clearly defined and well-implemented plan or those who may have drifted out of care in an unplanned way.[12] This is unfortunate because once a youngster has a "delinquent jacket" a couple of inches deep, it becomes extremely difficult to lose the label of serious or repeat offender and, often, to follow up that youngster. Simply put, their survival chances are cut in terms of making it on the outside in a nine-to-five world that is made for conformity, not deviance.

Our young men need to know that there are adults in the community to whom they can relate, from whom they can learn, and by whom they can be accepted and admired. St. Xavier's Boys' Home and Loyola House, where young men can come and be safe for a designated time in their lives, are significant. For some of these boys, this may well be the first time they experience security and consistency. Structured care plans, devised at the beginning of their stay and revised on a continuing basis, are essential if we are to equip these boys for their transition from care.

Notes

1. See Editor's Notes, this volume; McElwee, N. (2000). *To travel hopefully: Views from the managers of residential child care units in Ireland.* Kilkenny: Soc-Sci Press/RMA.

2. The official source of crime data in the Republic of Ireland is the Annual Report of the Garda Síochána (Irish police). These statistics are inevitably incomplete due to all crimes not being reported to and recorded by the police. Data on juvenile crime are available from the main records of crime held by the Garda Síochána and also from data on referrals to the National Juvenile Office, both of which are published in the Annual Report of the Garda Síochána.

3. Doob, A. N., & Cesaroni, C. (2004). *Responding to youth crime in Canada.* Toronto, ON: University of Toronto Press; Dooley, R., & Corbett, M. (2002). Child care, juvenile justice and the Children Act 2001. *Irish Youth Work Scene: A Journal for Youth Workers,* no. 36; Goldblatt, P., & Lewis, C. (1998). *Reducing offending: An assessment of research evidence on ways of dealing with offending behaviour.* London: Home Office; Dooley, R., & Corbett, M. (2002). Child care, juvenile justice and the Children Act 2001. *Irish Youth Work Scene: A Journal for Youth Workers,* no. 36; Goldblatt, P., & Lewis, C. (1998). *Reducing offending: An assessment of research evidence on ways of dealing with offending behaviour.* London: Home Office; Griffin, D. (2004). The juvenile conundrum: Ireland's responses to youth offending. *Cork Online Law Review* (3rd ed.). Retrieved June 21, 2004, from http://colr.ucc.ie/2004xii.html.

The vast majority of headline (indictable) offenses involving juveniles relate to crimes of larceny and burglary, with only a minute proportion involving offenses against the person. The most common nonheadline (nonindictable) offenses recorded against juveniles are criminal damage, public order, unauthorized taking or interference with vehicles, and traffic-related offenses.

The Children Act is framed on the generally accepted belief that the use of custody for children should be an option of last resort. It therefore places a strong emphasis on community interventions as a means to prevent offending and reoffending. *Irish Times,* March 31, 2004.

4. Child Care Act, 45,1,a. Dublin: Government Publications.

5. Irish Social Services Inspectorate. (2004). *Annual Report.* Dublin: Author, p. 4

6. Child Care Act. (1991). Dublin: Stationary Office.

7. Parents or guardians are obliged to be present at all court appearances relating to the child under the Children Act (2001). They are required to attend and participate if required in all stages of court proceedings against the child for an offense, relating to a family conference in respect of the child or to the failure of a child to comply with a community sanction. The court has the power to adjourn proceedings and issue a warrant for the arrest of the parents or guardian who fail to attend the court without reasonable excuse. Furthermore, their failure to attend is treated as if it were a contempt in the face of the court.

8. The Garda and the courts say that a hard core of young offenders is responsible for a large proportion of youth crime and that the lack of spaces in secure accommodation means many of the cases are struck out and offenders are released to continue reoffending. Gardaí believe many of these young people go on to become adult offenders. *Irish Times,* March 31, 2004.

9. Irish Social Services Inspectorate. (2006). *Annual Report.* Dublin: ISSI.

10. Wolberg, L. R. (1977). *The technique of psychotherapy.* New York: Grune & Stratton.
11. Altschuler, D. M., & Armstrong, T. L. (1999, July). Reintegrative confinement and intensive aftercare. *Juvenile Justice Bulletin,* 2–15.
12. *Irish Social Services Inspectorate.* (2006). Retrieved April 2006 from www.issi; O' Connor, M. (1998). *Children, young people and crime in Britain and Ireland: From exclusion to inclusion.* Stirling: Scottish Executive.

NIALL MCELWEE *is a senior lecturer in child and youth care and director of the Center for Child and Youth Care Learning in Athlone, Ireland.*

MICHAEL O'CONNOR *is assistant director of services, Focus Ireland.*

SUSAN MCKENNA *is with Relational Research & Consulting, Galway, Ireland.*

This chapter provides an overview of the development of legislation, policies, and practices in Scotland in relation to the transition from care to independent living.

7

The Scottish perspective: A pathway to progress?

Jeremy Millar

THE TRANSITION FROM a care setting to face the often grim realities of living more independently is arguably the most significant challenge that faces those who have been in public care and the workers offering them support. In the Scottish context, the past ten years have witnessed a growing awareness and engagement with this challenge, informed by some key pieces of research and significant legislative changes.

This chapter offers insight into the impact of the reforms in terms of direct work with care leavers in the northeast of Scotland and the broader aspirations of the new legislative framework. I begin with some historical context that links Scotland to the Commonwealth in terms of former child care practice and how this relates to societal and demographic changes. The response to the needs of children in the care of the state is still significantly influenced by the historical legacy and the manner in which this has impacts on the value base of key individuals involved in both direct care and policymaking in this field.

Go west, south, east . . .

Scotland in the nineteenth century was a harsh and unforgiving place for the majority of children to grow up in. Major social upheavals were in progress. The industrial revolution had resulted in an influx of poor rural families into the major cities and towns. Famine and endemic poverty in Ireland had resulted in the migration of many Irish families into Glasgow. These pressures on the poorly developed infrastructure and nonexistent social services created extreme conditions of deprivation, typified by:

- High infant mortality
- Chronic overcrowding and homelessness
- Epidemics of killer diseases and all-pervasive ill health
- Breakdown in family supports and community ties
- High incidence of alcohol misuse, mental health problems, and other related social ills
- Many children being placed at risk as a result of neglect, being orphaned, illegitimacy, and living in immoral surroundings

Until the mid-nineteenth century, the burden of caring for those children experiencing the effects of poverty, neglect, and abuse fell on the extended family and other supportive individuals and organizations within the immediate community. The introduction of the Poor Law (Scotland) Act 1845 saw the responsibility for welfare support fall on the local parish, with money collected by the congregations. Although theoretically this ensured a safety net, the entitlement rules excluded many of the most vulnerable. This disparity related directly to the concept of the deserving and undeserving poor. Children were viewed as deserving by merit of their age and vulnerability. However, their parents were judged far more harshly should they have resorted to the use of alcohol or the pursuit of an immoral lifestyle. I return to this concept in more detail later.

During the latter half of the nineteenth century, there emerged the provision of residential care for children. The philanthropic Victorian response was to rescue children and promote their welfare through a range of health- and education-based initiatives with a strong dose of moralizing and religious indoctrination.

Due to the extent of the poverty and the numbers of children coming to the attention of the authorities, it became apparent quickly that accommodating these children in purpose-built institutions was both costly and impractical. The innovative response was for many of these children to be dispatched to the colonies of the British Empire. This forced emigration of children from poor families was used by the resourceful Victorians to meet the need for labor in the emerging colonial countries. Many went to residential farm schools and orphanages. Lynn Abrams, in her authoritative book, *The Orphan Country*, suggests that between 1870 and 1930 around 80,000 to 100,000 British children were forcibly relocated to Canada alone.[1] In the Scottish context one organization, Quarriers Homes, sent 7,000 children overseas.

This policy is one telling element of the value that society placed on children who came into public care. The same judgments were attached to young people when it came to their moving on from the care setting. The strict hierarchies of the class system applied, with young women being prepared for service in the homes of the wealthy or local industry and young men prepared for the armed forces and manual labor on the land or in factories. However, this reality has to be viewed in the context of similar experiences for the vast majority of the working-class population for whom social mobility was not an option.

It is worth reflecting on the accumulative effect of displacement and enforced transition on families' sense of history and identity. There are some excellent oral history sources that complement the research of Abrams.[2] I strongly suspect that many workers in Commonwealth countries who have Scottish roots may have direct familial history that can connect them to the experience of the current generation of care leavers.

One further element to this historical perspective deserves mention, if only to flag the complex patterns of relationship that can serve to connect as much as they divide: the subsequent impact of the displaced young migrants on the lives of the indigenous peoples of the countries they settled in. The institutional measures taken to eradicate native cultures resonate with measures adopted against the poor in the United Kingdom of Great Britain.[3]

Left behind

In Scotland since the 1970s, there have been significant developments in terms of the evolution of class structures and social mobility. These can be characterized by the loss of the traditional industrial employment base, an increase in the numbers of young people leaving school to enter higher education, and a rise in the average age of leaving home. The current expectation in Scotland is that up to 50 percent of school leavers will go on to university, and many will remain at home until their mid-twenties. By contrast, only 1 percent of care leavers will go on to university, and the average age for leaving care is around sixteen.[4] This stark contrast emphasizes the extent to which young people who have been in public care are cast adrift in society. The increasing gulf between the most affluent and the poorest is clearly reflected in the experience of those leaving care.[5]

The poor outcomes for young care leavers in Scotland are evidenced in reduced life expectancy, increased mental health and general ill health problems, substance misuse and addiction problems, homelessness, admission to prison, and teenage pregnancy.[6]

Needs, not deeds

If there is one aspect of the Scottish philosophy in relation to children deemed to be at risk, it is the belief enshrined in the Social Work (Scotland) Act 1968 that the law should respond to children on the basis of their needs, not their deeds.[7] The practical application of this approach is most evident in the children's hearing system, established in 1971, in which a panel of laypeople determines, subject to background information and face-to-face questioning of social workers, the children, and their families, what would be in the child's best interests. Except for the most serious of offenses, this ensures that up to the age of at least sixteen, and technically to the age of eighteen, children and young people who commit offenses are not subject to a criminal justice system disposal.

This approach sits with the more enlightened Victorian philanthropic notion of rescuing children and attempting to distance them from the moral corruption often associated with their immediate environment. However, there exists an ongoing tension between the child-centered view of the legislation and the subsequent translation into practice.

You're on your own

This can be seen most clearly when young people reached the age of sixteen and were often discharged into the community with little awareness of their rights and entitlements in respect of ongoing support. If they had committed a criminal offense subsequent to their sixteenth birthday, it was often the case in my experience that judgments would be made as to the value of their facing the full weight of the adult criminal justice system, where they would be judged on their deeds, not their level of need.

I was privileged to run in the late 1980s a residential unit for young offenders, many of whom had been in care. The challenge was to keep them out of custody, and sometimes with the support of enlightened social workers, the legislation could be used to refer sixteen and seventeen year olds back to the children's hearing system and ensure that they didn't gain an adult criminal record. Sadly, the outcome was often less than positive. I can recall a number of young men from extremely deprived and abusive backgrounds who had been in the care of the state for the majority of lives ending up serving significant prison sentences as a result of their out-of-control offending behavior after they turned sixteen.

The received wisdom was that exposure to the possibility of a prison term would cause them to sort their lives out. As any experienced practitioner knows, it is the most damaged individuals for whom that sort of turnaround is least achievable without significant focused support. Unsurprisingly this was not forthcoming.

Another kind of home

It was becoming increasingly obvious that all-around provision for care leavers was failing to meet the complexity of individual need in the face of ongoing social upheaval. By the late 1980s and early 1990s, there was significant youth unemployment and homelessness that disproportionately hit the young people with care experiences. One further significant policy change linked to the government's view that family financial responsibility should be promoted was the withdrawal of benefit entitlement to sixteen and seventeen year olds. This policy change further stigmatized care leavers as they became subject to means testing in order to receive financial support from the state if they left care at age sixteen and seventeen.[8]

Around this time, there was a renewed focus on the standards of residential care provision for children and young people leading to the landmark report, *Another Kind of Home*.[9] Key recommendations in this report highlighted the need to view preparation for adulthood as a fundamental component of the care experience. The report also identified the benefits of young people being involved in the small decisions of everyday life, such as choice in relation to clothing, food purchasing, decor for their rooms, and undertaking leisure activities. The report recognizes the innovative work by some residential establishments in terms of providing what were called training flats, in which residents could practice their skills before moving on into more independent accommodation. Critical to this process is that the "encouragement to undertake these [tasks] and to provide support in making mistakes where necessary, is an important preparation for their future independence."[10]

Skinner reported that good practice was in evidence and characterized in the following ways:

- Young people moving on from stable care settings
- An acknowledgment from workers as to the emotional impact of the transition to more independent living on the young person
- Key workers maintaining contact after the move
- Young people being able to visit the residential unit after they had left
- Close attention being paid to community supports and the workers being enabled to work with supportive family members throughout the young person's journey through the care experience.
- Close links to providers of accommodation and the creation of a range of provision to meet differing needs
- A recognition of the particular needs of disabled young people in relation to their experience of the transition from children's services to adult provision
- Social work departments working to the spirit of the legislation to maximize support and opportunity for the care leaver

Before leaving this landmark document, it is worth sharing a further observation, made by the report, in relation to a holistic life cycle awareness seldom evidenced in strategic overviews. The report makes reference to adults returning to revisit the residential unit, perhaps when it is due for closure, and highlights the need for sensitive handling of the emotional issues for people at such times. This awareness of the importance of place, lived experience, and relationships with significant adults involved in their care is a theme that we cannot afford to overlook in a profession that is increasingly driven by performance indicators and outcomes.

Leaving residential care

The impact of reports such as *Another Kind of Home* fed into an overhaul of child care legislation in Scotland, resulting in the Children (Scotland) Act 1995 (CSA 1995).[11] The implementation of this new legal framework coincided with my move to take over management of a residential leaving-care project. I inherited a project that met some of the considerations for good practice Skinner identified but also fell short in the area of being aspirational in the promotion of increased opportunity for young people in care.

Aspiration and inspiration

There was in a sense some legacy of the Victorian values around the response to the deserving and undeserving poor. An example might be around an assumption that we should not spend time supporting a young woman into a career, as she will only get pregnant to some "waster" and end up like her mother. This resignation to an acceptance of people remaining on the bottom rung of the social order was closely linked to some staff members' own working-class experiences. Coming as I did from an educated middle-class background, I struggled to accept the worldview presented to me. There was a significant clash of cultural expectations closely linked to the aspirational agenda.

The process of informing and educating staff about different practices, values, and aspirations unfortunately led to the shedding of half the workforce and the introduction of fresh young faces possessing a social work qualification. There is no firm evidence to link better practice to the staff qualifications,[12] but in terms of how the ethos within the unit is developed, it is useful to have people able to practice reflectively with a working knowledge of child development. A further advantage in bringing in newly qualified young workers was to create a learning culture that modeled possibilities for the resident group. It does, however, sharply highlight the potential for a class-based divide among the staff group that once again resonates with many of the nineteenth-century themes of rescue and the imposition of the dominant ideological values.

One young woman aspired to be a journalist and enjoyed discussing and debating with staff on issues of the day. She clearly gravitated to workers who could engage and meet this need to challenge and explore her developing ideas. It was interesting to observe in team meetings how staff interpreted her behavior, with some criticizing her for being oppositional and disrespectful and others viewing her as stimulating and fun to be around. It is with some satisfaction that I can recount that she went on to become one of the youngest lay members of the children hearing system and now works with young people in a community project within an inner-city area of deprivation. She has children, is happily married, and continues to work with her feelings and experiences of being in care. I am acutely aware of how it could have been so different if key workers had not been there to hang out and hang in with her.

Corporate parenting

The CSA 1995 introduces the concept of corporate parenting. At-risk children become looked after by the local authority, and the authority has a duty to safeguard and promote their welfare. It is also the authorities' duty to provide advice and assistance in preparing children for the time when they are no longer looked after. The significant shift in perception here is the move from viewing the promotion of the child's welfare as the exclusive role of the social work and social service agency to one where the entire resources of the local authority are theoretically available to promote the child's best interests.

In Scotland, a local authority has responsibility for providing a range of public services. Crucially, for children, these include education, social work, public housing, leisure, and recreation. When it comes to a young person moving on from being looked after by the local authority, there are specific references in the CSA 1995 to providing aftercare in some form until the age of twenty-one. This duty extends to the completion of further or higher education courses even if the courses extend beyond the age of twenty-one.[13]

This is all well and good, but a lot can get lost in the translation, and the people's core values play a significant role. Returning now to my own practice experience, at the project for care leavers, I will describe some aspects of these tensions. I inherited a team, some of whom had been in their post for many years in traditional children's homes and displayed many of the characteristics of institutionalized practice. Some staff members resented or failed to understand the significance of the transition that the young person was about to make. There were comments regularly made about the level of support from some staff members being too high, with, for example, young people being encouraged by their key worker to phone the unit if they were in difficulty. It therefore became a lottery for the care leaver as to whether he or she received an understanding response or a dismissive reaction when contacting the unit.

Taking a psychosocial perspective and drawing on an understanding of working in the life space, we attempted as a staff team to explore the meanings contained in the process of moving on from care for the young person, their families, and ourselves as a staff group. With some staff members, I had a constant challenge to engage them with reflection on loss in their own lives and unresolved injustices they had perhaps experienced at the hands of caregivers and the educational system.

At the extremes, I had one staff member who never ventured willingly from the office into face-to-face contact with the residents and another who would happily construct the day around a succession of visits to ex-residents living in the community, barely touching down in the unit. Understandably both these individuals' behaviors caused a degree of upset through their approach to the task.

Contrasts in the corporate approach

The practice of moving out of residential care at that time was extremely difficult to characterize. I will describe a best possible scenario and one where I believe we failed a young person significantly. I will use these examples from the late 1990s and early 2000s to demonstrate how the shortcomings in the system fed into the reviewed and revised position we have currently.

A young person in public care is subject to regular review as a looked-after child. This would happen at six-month intervals unless there were significant changes in their circumstances requiring prompt discussion. The reviews would involve the young person, key family members or other supportive adults, and the relevant professionals involved in their care. The residential key worker would have a crucial role in coordinating the care plan and updating other individuals in the young person's life. This person would have by far the most contact with the young person and would plan the move in detail with the young person.

The support of the young person would encompass discussing and gaining a sense of the best time to move on. They would look with the young person at other stresses in life such as exams, starting work, or the coming Christmas holiday. There would be discussion around who should be involved in the move. Often this was a time when family members wanted to become involved and acknowledge the transition, hoping often that their child would get a better start in adult life than they had. The assistance might range from financial assistance to practical help decorating the new home. The young person would be experiencing within the residential home a range of new experiences linked to becoming more independent. These opportunities would cover symbolic actions such as getting a front door key to the unit and the removal of curfews that applied to younger members of the resident group. Also, practical task-oriented experiences were related to shopping, budgeting, cooking, and cleaning. The idea was that staff members would model desired behavior and pass on the wisdom of their own transition experiences.

One crucial element of good practice would be the discussion around the imminent new reality, the rehearsing of what to do in worrisome situations, and the acknowledgment of those areas in which we, as the corporate parent, would struggle to meet their needs. The loneliness encountered by everyone on first settling into a new flat is a good example of this. The security elicited from the committed relationship with the key worker and other staff members with the certain knowledge that the door is always open cannot be underestimated at this stage.

The length of the follow-up support should be driven by need rather than some notion of a staged reduction in contact in order to avoid creating an unhealthy dependency. It is interesting to reflect on how the findings of Goffman[14] in relation to loss of identity in large institutions has been co-opted to the cause of promoting a notion of some achievable level of independence in the community. It is more useful to engage with the notion of interdependence throughout the life cycle, coupled with an awareness of the impact of loss and the psychosocial need to retreat to safe places with trusted people who can assist in the containment of the pain found in those moments. Jim Anglin[15] talks powerfully on this topic, and Jo Dixon and Mike Stein[16] offer the views of Scottish young people on what makes for good support in the postcare world. They talk powerfully of being caught up in rejecting the guidance of the adults when moving on at age sixteen to eighteen and realizing with hindsight that these adults did in fact have their best interests at heart. Those who had ongoing supports to whom they could turn when things got difficult highlighted how important this was for them.

In terms of the corporate parent role, it was the enlightened practice in the local authority that I worked for to offer access to quality accommodation through a consortium of housing providers who would interview the young person to establish his or her own preferences in relation to this first home. This would take into account the closeness to community supports, employment, and avoidance of negative influences such as previous relationships with those involved in drug use. In addition, the young person would be entitled to a nonmeans-tested grant of £1,750 to furnish and equip the flat. The young person would be fully involved in the choosing of the furnishings and the decor, promoting a sense of ownership.

I have just described the experience of young people moving on in a planned manner with the full support and cooperation of family and professionals alike. They will have had the ability to exercise choice in key decisions, such as the time to move and the accommodation that they move into. They will have been offered practical and financial resources and, most important, open access to the support of trusted adults and a staged transition from the residential unit with an allowance made for a return in times of difficulty. It is this type of transition that sits well with the findings of the Skinner report.

The commitment to this model of best practice was achieved on many occasions, but the reality for many others was less well thought through and planned. It is with the benefit of hindsight that I can identify how we failed the more vulnerable individuals due to our inability to recognize the messages coming from our own assessment, coupled with that of our perverse ability to reject our understanding of child development, attachment, and resilience and retreat into the blaming and labeling behavior of determined behaviorists.

One young man of Pakistani birth came to our unit following the breakdown of foster care placement. This young man had both a physical disability and a learning disability. In terms of vulnerability, he was by our assessment at significant risk of a range of potentially exploitive and abusive relationships. We did well in terms of engaging him in positive relationships within the group living situation, and we were proud of the work we did to help him explore his sense of identity as a black youth of Pakistani origin. There were plans afoot to assist him into supported employment in a community project. What we failed to address was the protection afforded this young man through the legal system. He was approaching age eighteen and no longer subject to the supervision of the children's hearing system. He had been kept under supervision out of concern for his well-being. There is a process for adult measures of guardianship that can be implemented for vulnerable adults.[17] Before we could initiate an application for these measures, the young man had been contacted by relatives in England with an invitation to join them on a visit to relatives in Pakistan. He was excited by this prospect, and with the assistance of his former foster carers, he left the area. After this, we attempted to retrieve the situation by contacting the social services in the area he had traveled to in England. There was no contact, and it is my understanding that he returned to Pakistan.

The lesson here for me was about the holistic planning process and working through the complex assumptions, both cultural and disability related, that confront us in cases where we as workers are out of our professional comfort zone. Lessons such as these were apparent throughout the practice of throughcare and aftercare since the introduction of the CSA 1995. The next section examines the evolution of the existing policies for young people leaving care in Scotland.

"Still a bairn?"

There is a powerful narrative developing that acknowledges the voices of those who have received social work services.[18] In respect of care leavers in Scotland, the landmark report is a piece of research undertaken by the University of York for the Scottish Executive.[19] It begins with the following quote from a young woman identified as Heather: "I'm only 16 and still a bairn and get a bit weepy at times." From this quote comes the title of the report. *Still a Bairn?* (*bairn* being the Scottish word for child). Heather is referring to fear felt in being expected to move on from care at age sixteen. Dixon and Stein surveyed thirty-one of the thirty-two Scottish local authorities and spoke to key policymakers, managers, frontline staff, and young people over a two-year period between 2000 and 2002. They presented a comprehensive view of the intention, practice, and reality of the delivery of throughcare and aftercare services to Scotland's looked-after population of children and young people, of whom around thirteen hundred move on each year.

The report found that 77 percent of local authorities offered planned throughcare programs, but only 39 percent of young people had received one. In addition, only 60 percent of young people had had a formal leaving-care review. There were significant variations in service provision across authorities, with a generally low level of monitoring and evaluation of the effectiveness of services. It was noted that most authorities had a commitment to involving young people in the development and evaluation of services.

In terms of outcomes for young people, the report notes the extremely poor educational outcomes, with nearly two-thirds leaving full-time compulsory schooling with no qualifications at all. Also of concern was the lack of knowledge displayed by workers in relation to the educational achievements of those they were supporting. One-quarter professed to have no knowledge. This is a significant finding in terms of my own practice observations around workers modeling a learning culture and promoting an aspirational environment.

Reflecting directly the findings of the Skinner report ten years earlier, Dixon and Stein found evidence of the negative impact of multiple placement moves, with one-third experiencing four or more moves and only 7 percent remaining in the same placement throughout their care history. A summary of the report states, "Reliable support, whether formal or informal, was paramount to positive outcomes in most life areas and the ability to access and return to services when in need was crucial for young people finding their way through the challenges of post care living."[20]

The findings of *Still a Bairn* fed into a review undertaken by a working group on the throughcare and aftercare of looked-after children in Scotland.[21] They recommended the following key points:

- Local authorities should have in place systems for accurately recording the numbers of eligible young people requiring support.
- There should be a plan in place for each young person leaving care.
- There should be an identified lead person for each young person leaving care.
- Local authorities should know the destination, accommodation arrangements, and number of moves and any periods of homelessness for each care leaver.
- Local authorities should know the education, employment, and training status of those receiving aftercare.
- There should be a comprehensive assessment process for each young person.
- The financial responsibility for the young person should rest with the local authority until the young person reaches age eighteen.
- There should be a system in place for the young person to seek speedy resolution to any complaint over the level of service.

These recommendations are now embedded in the legal framework through the Supporting Young People in Scotland: Regulations and Guidance on the Services for Young People Ceasing to be Looked After by Local Authorities.[22] For the most authoritative account of the process and the current situation, I recommend the book *Leaving Care: Throughcare and Aftercare in Scotland*.[23]

A pathway to progress?

One key element of the changes to throughcare and aftercare provision is the development and adoption of an assessment tool referred to as Pathways.[24] This framework has been developed with significant involvement from young people and has attempted to build on and dovetail with the existing looked-after children assessment and recording materials. One exciting aspect of this tool is the fact that while retaining the fundamental purpose, a number of local authorities have adapted the document following consultation with young people. At least one authority has developed an electronic version that the young person can work on at his or her own pace, removing the often intrusive element of an unfamiliar person asking questions.

The Pathways materials serve to establish and record key personal information and the responsibilities of the support team. Importantly it elicits the views of the young person in respect of these life dimensions:

- Lifestyle
- Family and friends
- Health and well-being
- Learning and work
- Where I live
- Money
- Rights and legal issues

Crucially it also records hopes for the future, introducing that missing element of the aspirational. It offers the opportunity to describe goals and obstacles in relation to achieving objectives detailed in the life dimensions. Caution has to be expressed for reasons previously stated in respect to staff motivation and their valuing of such a tool.

In answering many of the concerns highlighted by previous research, the new procedures offer a level of involvement and accountability that should provide the young person with support financially, emotionally, and practically up to the age of at least eighteen and beyond, to age twenty-one in many cases. The fact that the financial maintenance of the young person rests with the local authority until the person attains the age of eighteen should prevent him or her from being let go of at sixteen, disappearing from sight, and often to reappear in adult criminal justice and mental health systems. The process of encouraging culture change among providers, residential child care workers, and the young people and their families will take time and leadership.

In an attempt to gauge how far down this route Scotland's local authorities were one year after implementation, I undertook a survey of the perceptions of the lead officers, in each of the authorities, who were charged with driving implementation.[25] Out of thirty-two authorities, seventeen replied, with 85 percent stating that they had a dedicated throughcare and aftercare service.

Respondents were offered the opportunity to rate themselves on a scale that progressed from "nowhere near," through "struggling," "hopeful signs," "getting there," "quietly confident," " arriving at," to "completely sorted." In the Scottish culture, it is unlikely for people to shout about their success from the rooftop, so "getting there" and "quietly confident" probably represent significant progress. Using this scale, it was clear that 75 percent felt they were making good progress one year on. This view also applied to the adoption of the Pathways materials. The views expressed made reference to staff resistance and the challenge of corporate culture change. Some officers reported that young people had been resistant to using the Pathways, feeling that they had grown out of the system. This resistance had initiated some of the innovative work to develop the materials into a more user-friendly form. Further feedback on Pathways referred to the challenge of maintaining it as a living document rather than a procedural requirement. It was no surprise that the most progress had been made in relation to the legal responsibility to have financial supports in place.

"Getting there"

Transitions provoke strong emotional responses, bringing into sharp relief previous loss, excitement over future opportunity, and realizing hidden potential. In this process, residential child care and aftercare support workers have a key role to direct and facilitate much of the process. A keen understanding of both their own history and that of the individuals they work with and their communities is essential in order to engage with the elements of shared humanity and common experience, avoiding the reduction of the process to one of procedure evidenced by the mechanistic, sometimes literal, checking off of boxes. In the Scottish context, there is a time line of tension between ways of working that start with a child in need and a commitment to betterment through the provision of opportunity and one that reverts to a judgmental position that assumes worthiness of investment being predicated on a complex equation of the worker's personal history of opportunity, the child's deeds, and whether they demonstrate gratitude, class-based assumptions, and agency culture.

The structures that we have developed moving into the twenty-first century offer a value base that is clearly aspirational and can be constructively used to promote opportunities for growth, safety, and ongoing nurturing relationships. The challenge remains one of both personal and organizational cultural change.

Notes

1. Abrams, L. (1998) *The orphan country*. Edinburgh: John Donald Publishers. This is the authoritative book on the history of child welfare and protection in Scotland.

2. www.bbc.co.uk/radio4/history/child_migrants.shtml. This oral history features child migrants in Australia. It is available to listen to online.

3. An informative and moving article by Pemina Yellow Bird on the treatment of Native peoples within the U.S. psychiatric system is *Wild Indians: Native perspectives on the Hiawatha Asylum for Insane Indians*. Retrieved August 28, 2006, from http://www.patdeegan.com/pdfs/PeminasManuscript.pdf.

4. Dixon, J., & Stein, M. (2002). *"Still a bairn?" Throughcare and aftercare services in Scotland.* Retrieved August 28, 2006, from www.scotland.gov.uk.
5. *Changing lives: Report of the 21st century social work review.* (2006). Edinburgh: Scottish Executive. Retrieved February 2, 2007, from http://www.scotland.gov.uk/Publications/2006/02/02094408/0.
6. Dixon & Stein. (2002). See also Broad, B. (2005), *Improving the health and wellbeing of young people leaving care.* Lyme Regis: Russell House Publishing.
7. Social Work Scotland Act. (1968).
8. Social Security Act. (1986). This legislation removed entitlement to certain benefits for sixteen and seventeen year olds.
9. Skinner, A. (1992). *Another kind of home: A review of residential child care.* Edinburgh: Scottish Office.
10. Skinner. (1992).
11. Children (Scotland) Act. (1995).
12. Berridge, D. (1997). *Children's homes revisited.* London: Jessica Kingsley.
13. Children (Scotland) Act 1995 HMSO. Sections 29 and 30 of the legislation deal with throughcare and aftercare support and continuing education.
14. Goffman, E. (1961). *Asylums.* New York: Doubleday.
15. Anglin, J. (2002). *Pain, normality, and the struggle for congruence.* New York: Haworth Press.
16. Dixon, J., & Stein, M. (2005). *Leaving care; Throughcare and aftercare in Scotland.* London: Jessica Kingsley. This is the book based on the research contained in the *"Still a bairn"* report.
17. Adults with Incapacity (Scotland) Act. (2000).
18. *Changing lives.* (2006).
19. Dixon & Stein. (2002). This report draws heavily on the voices of young people.
20. Dixon & Stein. (2002).
21. *Throughcare and aftercare of looked after children in Scotland.* (2002). London: HMSO.
22. Dixon, J., & Stein, M. *Supporting young people leaving care in Scotland: Regulations and guidance on services for young people ceasing to be looked after by local authorities.* (2004). Edinburgh: Scottish Executive.
23. Dixon & Stein. (2005).
24. www.scottishthroughcare.org.uk. The Pathways materials can be accessed through this site, along with a range of resources in relation to throughcare and aftercare.
25. Unpublished research I undertook in 2005.

JEREMY MILLAR *is a lecturer at the Robert Gordon University/The Scottish Institute for Residential Childcare in Aberdeen, Scotland.*

This chapter explores the benefits of engaging youth as resources in all levels of child welfare work. The respect inherent in this inclusion not only assists the development of a stronger bond between youth and staff, it also results in more effective policies, programs, and services.

8

Using youth expertise at all levels: The essential resource for effective child welfare practice

Kathi M. Crowe

THE PAST TWO DECADES have seen remarkable advances in the manner in which youth are transitioned out of the foster care system. The most significant progress is in the way that the child welfare system relates to the youth it serves. This chapter provides a contextual framework for the advances in child welfare's preparation of youth for self-sufficiency and highlights the evidence and benefits of a significant cultural shift away from "doing for" toward "doing with" youth in foster care. The embracing of youth as partners, not only in individual case planning but also in the development, implementation, and evaluation of policies, programs, and services, has resulted in tremendous gains for the profession as well as the youth. This chapter illustrates those gains on both the micro and macro levels and suggests some critical ingredients that ensure that the expertise of youth is used appropriately and thoughtfully.

Advances in the independent living field

We have witnessed increased federal support for the provision of independent living and transitional services for youth through the passage in 1999 of the Foster Care Independence Act which established the John H. Chafee Foster Care Independence Program,[1] the development of innovative transitional housing models,[2] a variety of excellent tools for the assessment and development of life skill competencies, and policies and protocols at the state and local levels that require the demonstration of efforts aimed at ensuring a successful transition. We have also seen more meaningful collaboration on the part of providers of independent living and transitional living services to youth. Opportunities for sharing best practices have increased with the convening of more frequent and larger conferences and organizations, such as the National Independent Living Association and the National Foster Care Coalition, and brought needed focus to the plight and needs of older youth who are exiting the foster care system. Awareness of the needs and concerns of foster children and youth has also been heightened by the annual National Foster Care Month campaign, conducted in May.[3] All of these components combine to enhance the service delivery system for older youth, but perhaps no other component has affected the system itself more significantly than the manner in which that system relates to youth.

Positive youth development

The most significant advance in the field of independent living and transitional living services is embracing an approach to working with youth. That approach has been labeled differently as it has expanded and matured over many years. Initially included as part of a larger concept of youth empowerment, the embracing of youth as partners is an essential component of the concept currently referred to as positive youth development. Although the approach is widely endorsed and promoted within the child welfare community, it did not originate there. In the 1970s, the Department of

Health, Education and Welfare established the National Youth Development Bureau, which established state and regional bureaus across the United States. In the early 1990s, the DeWitt-Wallace Foundation funded projects throughout the country through character-building organizations such as the YMCA, Boys and Girls Clubs of America, Boy and Girl Scouts, and the National 4-H program, which promoted concepts of youth empowerment through the National Collaboration for Youth.

The Child Welfare League of America (CWLA) joined the National Collaboration in 1992, becoming a DeWitt-Wallace grantee, and introduced the concept of positive youth development to the child welfare community. Through the positive youth development training curriculum and other materials, the Child Welfare League advanced the practice of including youth as partners in child welfare policy and practice. This philosophy has been widely accepted as best practice for working with youth in a variety of arenas and has been increasingly embraced within the child welfare community.

The Child Welfare League of America, in its 2005 Standards of Excellence for Transition, Independent Living and Self-Sufficiency Services (TILSS), established positive youth development philosophy as the foundation for TILSS services. It describes positive youth development programs as focused on the strengths and potential of youth rather than their problems or deficits and declares that TILSS programs and services should include (among other things) "structured and ongoing opportunities for youth to participate in leadership, decision-making, policy and program development, evaluation, and peer assistance."[4]

In the 1980s, youth engagement was largely restricted to participation in youth advisory boards.[5] These boards appeared on the child welfare landscape on many levels. State governments began developing youth advisory boards as part of their independent living programs. Unfortunately, while most states wanted a youth advisory board and appreciated the potential value such a group could offer to the agency, many states did not operationalize the boards in a manner to ensure their success.

Often these boards were poorly supported and understaffed by child welfare professionals who received little to no training on board or youth development and already felt burdened by a full cadre of responsibilities. Realistic arrangements for practical aspects such as the scheduling of and transportation of youth to board meetings and the provision of food at the meetings were not considered. Often there were inadequate budgets for the completion of projects that youth wanted to initiate and little advance guidance regarding what projects would be endorsed. Youth frequently felt like tokens instead of partners who were being used to their full potential. Many states had no clear process for the nomination or selection of youth to the board, resulting in selection by favoritism, and a perspective skewed by including only youth who had managed to do relatively well in the system. Other states attempted to mandate participation on the board or brought youth to meetings with little or no preparation. As a result, states often had difficulty maintaining their youth advisory boards and experienced frequent turnover and inertia.

Private agencies providing services to older youth also began developing youth advisory boards, often with similar results. Selection of board members was frequently done by staff rather than by peers, which led to boards that were not representative of the thoughts and feelings of the majority of youth in the programs. Again, training of staff and youth regarding board development was lacking, and the result often was frequent turnover of youth board members as well as staff facilitators and dramatically underused boards.

Beyond youth advisory boards

We have moved far beyond the approach of isolating youth feedback into limited and narrow youth advisory boards that allow the input of only a few hand-selected youth. Increasingly, care is being taken to ensure that youth advisory boards are representative of the diversity of youth in care. The composition of the board is critical, and care must be taken to ensure that the recruiting process results in a board that reflects the demographics of the youth served by the agency in terms of culture, gender, mix of urban and rural experiences, and experience with the range of programs and services offered by the agency, including shelters, foster homes, group homes, residential treatment, adoption, and juvenile correctional facilities. Nomination and selection criteria should be established to ensure that youth are endorsed by their peers. Care should also be taken to ensure that the thoughts and ideas of the larger group of youth are reflected in the projects and activities of the board. This has successfully been accomplished by conducting youth board-led focus groups and surveys and placing suggestion boxes in places where youth have access, which are collected and responded to by the youth advisory board.[6]

Also essential to a successful youth advisory board is access to decision makers within and outside the agency. Commissioners and key leaders of public and private child welfare agencies should meet regularly with the boards to elicit feedback from the youth on issues and initiatives and to hear from the youth concerns and suggestions.

As state and private child welfare agencies have gained experience with the development and support of youth advisory boards, the roles of the boards have been greatly broadened, and many successful boards have evolved that are truly representative of youth-driven organizations. They have been active in legislative advocacy on state and national levels and have successfully lobbied for the passage of major reforms and initiatives, including legislation that provides tuition assistance and tuition waivers to many higher education institutions.

Coordinated efforts of youth-led organizations are credited with contributing greatly to the passage of the Chafee Foster Care Independence Program in 1999. The California Youth Connection (CYC) is a premier example of an organization that is truly youth driven.[7] Established in 1988, the CYC is organized into local chapters throughout the state and has made great strides to network with California's foster youth. In addition to holding annual statewide conferences for foster youth, CYC has been active in legislative advocacy and has been holding an annual "Day at the Capitol" since 1993, when youth tour the capitol, meet with key legislators and their staff, and hold a press conference highlighting the concerns of foster youth. In 2000, CYC successfully advocated for legislation that requires the participation of foster youth in the development of child welfare policy and identifies CYC as the vehicle for that input. The organization has established such credibility that in California, it is now considered standard operating procedure, whenever there are child welfare reform efforts or planning activities, to reserve a place at the table for CYC representatives.

The practice of using youth as partners has resulted in numerous benefits to youth, the adults who work with youth, and the systems that provide services and develop policies. Increased voluntary program participation, decreased resistance, improved communication, and improved relationships between youth and social service staff are among the positive results being demonstrated through stronger partnerships. Developing meaningful ways for youthful consumer voices to be integrated into individual casework as well as into the development, implementation, and evaluation of services helps to ensure that services are appropriately designed and implemented and that resistance is minimized.

The business community has been using consumer feedback in the design and marketing of products for decades, conducting focus groups, surveys, and other measures to predict and respond to customer preferences and market trends. The social service industry in general, including child welfare, has historically maintained full control and responsibility for the design of services. This approach has led to a back-end, or trial-and-error, method of service delivery and program development, adjusting and revising program models after the fact as they prove ineffective or underused. Older youth in the child welfare system often refuse to comply with case plans that do not reflect their desires and are hesitant to participate in programs that they had no part in selecting. Historically, professionals have responded with attaching the label of "resistant" to these youth, in effect, blaming the youth for their reluctance to participate in a system in which they had no voice. This adds one more label to youth who have frequently accumulated several negative labels by the time they reach adolescence. This continuation of negative labeling is in direct opposition to a positive youth development, or strength-based, approach.

More effective than the trial-and-error method of program development is the meaningful inclusion of youth in the front end of service design, at both the micro and macro levels.

Including youth at the micro level of service design

On the micro level, youth are more actively being engaged in the development of their case plans. Best practice demands that youth are true partners in the development of the plans from their outset rather than the earlier practice of having social caseworkers write the plans and then asking youth to sign off on them, with little or no input. The Foster Care Independence Act mandates youth participation in the development of their transition plans. An essential component to engaging youth as partners in the case planning process is to ensure that they are available to attend all case planning reviews, court hearings, and meetings where decisions are being made. This involves practical considerations such as scheduling meetings at times and locations accessible to youth. The business hours of most child welfare agencies do not easily accommodate meetings that are scheduled around youth's school and work responsibilities. This conflict places youth in the difficult position of having to choose between fulfilling educational and employment responsibilities, sharing personal information regarding their status as a foster child to get the time out of school or time off from work, or missing meetings where important decisions regarding their life will be made without their input or presence. For older youth transitioning to economic self-sufficiency, unpaid hours taken out of work can sabotage fragile budgets and jeopardize employment.

Another recent development in the delivery of child welfare services has advanced the practice of youth partnership. Many states have extended services to youth beyond the age of eighteen, often including young adults up to age twenty-one. Some states continue eligibility beyond age twenty-one to students attending full-time higher educational or vocational training programs. Given that the legal emancipation age in most states remains eighteen, expanding services beyond that is done on a voluntary basis. This phenomenon has resulted in the development of services that must be delivered in a manner appealing to voluntary consumers. Youth who, when they were under age eighteen, were legally mandated to comply with services, suddenly at age eighteen are empowered to either reject services and become independent or accept services. For these older youth to want to continue to participate in child welfare services, the services must be designed and delivered in ways that are beneficial and respectful. The services developed for this age group are being designed to meet important needs in a consumer-friendly manner. Aftercare services are also being developed that do not require older youth to remain on full-time child welfare caseloads to be able to access needed services.

Including youth at the macro level of planning

Youth are increasingly being asked to participate in system-level reform and initiatives. The U.S. Department of Health and Human Services, Administration of Families, Children's Bureau, uses foster youth in the evaluation of child welfare services during its child and family service reviews. The Child Welfare League of America includes foster youth and alumni in all of its committees and work groups, and it has several former foster care youth serving on its board of directors. Youth are developing and reviewing curriculum used to train child welfare professionals and foster parents and are being used to conduct preservice and in-service training sessions. Youth in foster care are reviewing policies and providing feedback on program proposals and grant applications.

Youth are providing workshops and conducting keynote presentations at local and national conferences. One innovative national organization, FosterClub, provides leadership development to an elite group of current and former foster youth who have been selected through a nomination and application process to participate in a program called the Foster Club All Stars.[8] These young adults, aged eighteen through twenty-two, participate in a rigorous summer internship during which they develop their leadership and public speaking skills. They then apply those skills throughout the year, providing workshops, keynote addresses, panel facilitation, and managing youth conferences across the country.[9]

Other national organizations working within the child welfare field have established positions on their boards of directors specifically designated for current and former foster youth. One of the first such organizations was the National Independent Living Association, which established that policy in its by-laws in 1995.[10] The by-laws of the National Foster Care Coalition, established in 2005, also reserve positions on its board of directors for the voice of foster youth and alumni.[11] A new national organization, Foster Care Alumni of America, established in 2005, is committed to transforming foster care policy and practice by linking and organizing the foster care alumni community. Most members of the board of directors are foster care alumni.

Cautions and challenges

The child welfare system still has much work to do as it develops more and better ways to fully use youth expertise. Careful consideration must be given to ensure that mutual benefits are derived and that youth are not taken advantage of while being engaged in system reforms. Since older youth are appropriately concerned with securing their own futures, child welfare professionals who wish to use their time must consider the impact on the youth's education and employment goals. Compensation should be provided to youth who are participating in activities designed to improve the child welfare system. They should be treated as young consultants and provided emotional support, career advancement opportunities, and monetary compensation. It is also important not to overrely on particular youth who need to focus on establishing their own self-sufficiency plans. Youth often have charitable inclinations and genuinely want to help to improve the child welfare system, but they should not be expected, or even encouraged, to make sacrifices that will jeopardize their own security. It is the responsibility of child welfare professionals to ensure that youth are utilized without being used.

Transportation must be provided when appropriate and arrangements made so that youth do not have to pay for travel and other expenses and then wait for lengthy reimbursement processes. If youth are expected to travel to conferences or distant meetings, responsible and appropriate arrangements should be made for someone to meet or accompany them.

Another frequently cited obstacle is appropriate concern about confidentiality. States and agencies need to develop clear guidelines regarding youth being photographed and telling their stories to the public. Many states use alumni or youth over the age of majority to overcome this obstacle.

Conclusion

The depth and breadth of youth involvement in the planning, delivery, and evaluation of child welfare services is destined to expand as increasing numbers of government and private agencies experience the benefits of having meaningful and genuine partnerships with youth. The honesty and clarity that youthful voices provide have made a significant impact on child welfare in general and especially on the field of independent living and transitional living. Future generations of children and youth as well as child welfare professionals owe much to the contributions of the youth who have come before them.

Notes

1. The John H. Chafee Foster Care Independence Program was established in Title I of the Foster Care Independence Act (P.L.106–169). Retrieved February 7, 2005, from http://www.access.gpo.gov/nara/publaw/106pub.html. Pub.L.106–169 (H.R. 3443).

2. Kroner, M. J. (1999). *Housing options for independent living programs: Youth work resources.* Washington, DC: CWLA Press.

3. Casey Family Programs. (2005). *It's my life: Housing, a guide for transition services from Casey Family Programs.* Seattle. WA: Author.

4. Child Welfare League of America. (2005). *Standards of excellence for transition, independent living, and self-sufficiency services.* Washington, DC: Author.

5. Center for the Study of Social Policy. (2003, February). *Policy matters: Setting and measuring benchmarks for state policies, engaging youth in positive and productive roles: Recommendations for state policy.* Washington, DC: Author.

6. Crowe, K. M. (2001). Utilizing youth at all levels. *Common Ground, 17*(1).
7. Scott, P., Sanchez, R., & Grice, M. (N.d.). *A summary of foster youth recommendations from California Youth Connection Conferences.* Unpublished manuscript.
8. www.fosterclub.org, a Web site for supportive adults.
9. www.fyi3.com. This is the Web site for youth transitioning from foster care.
10. www.NILA.org.
11. www.NFCC.org.

KATHI M. CROWE *is a consultant to the National Independent Living Association in Rhode Island.*

Afterword: Aging out of care—Toward realizing the possibilities of emerging adulthood

Jeffrey Jensen Arnett

THE PREVIOUS CHAPTERS in this volume effectively portray the difficulties that young people face when they age out of care. Across countries and across regions of the United States, the pattern is similar: aging out of care means entering a high-risk period for numerous problems, including homelessness, unemployment, substance abuse, incarceration, and mental health difficulties.

As a developmental psychologist, I approach the issue of aging out of care from a somewhat different perspective than the social work perspective that is the basis for most of the previous chapters. In this chapter, I articulate the developmental issues that pertain to the late teens through the twenties and how these issues apply to aging out of care.

As the other chapter authors observe, it takes longer today for young people to reach a stable young adult living situation than it did in the past. Because the economies in industrialized countries have shifted from a manufacturing base to an information and technology base in recent decades, more education and training are required than in the past to obtain a desirable job.[1] Median ages of entering marriage and parenthood have risen steeply over the past half-century, into at least the late twenties in every industrialized country.[2] Furthermore, most young people today have mixed feelings about reaching adulthood.[3] They are in no hurry to make the transition to adulthood but prefer to take on adult responsibilities gradually in the course of their twenties, as they feel ready for them.

I have argued that the transition to adulthood has become so long in industrialized societies that it is necessary to recognize that a new phase of the life course has been created, which I have termed *emerging adulthood*.[4] People used to go from adolescence to young adulthood in their late teens or very early twenties, when they chose a stable occupation, married, and had their first child. Now, most people experience adolescence, then emerging adulthood, then young adulthood. Emerging adulthood lasts from the late teens (beginning about age eighteen) through at least the mid-twenties.

In terms of normative development, emerging adulthood has five features that distinguish it from the adolescence that proceeds it or the young adulthood that follows it.[5] Emerging adulthood is the age of identity explorations, the age of instability, the self-focused age, the age of feeling in between, and the age of possibilities. These are not features that exist only in emerging adulthood, but they are more pronounced in emerging adulthood than at other ages.

The five features have received empirical support as characterizing normative development in emerging adulthood.[6] However, emerging adulthood is also notable for its heterogeneity. It is the time when people's lives are least likely to be structured by social institutions.[7] Children's and adolescents' lives are structured by family and school, and adults lives (in young adulthood and after) by family and work. However, emerging adults typically move away from their families, and their school and work patterns tend to be relatively unstructured and unstable. Consequently, one of the most important tasks for the new field of emerging adulthood is to explore the heterogeneity that exists among emerging adults, especially the nonnormative patterns they may follow.

Emerging adults who have aged out of care are an important part of this heterogeneity. The challenges facing them, and their limited resources for facing those challenges, are evident in the preceding chapters. To what extent do the five features presented above apply to them? Are there other developmental issues that may apply to them? These are the questions I address here.

The age of identity explorations

In Erikson's theory of development across the life span, identity is the primary challenge of adolescence.[8] Adolescence is the age when people evaluate their abilities, interests, and identifications with important adults, then use this knowledge as a basis for making enduring decisions in the areas of love, work, and ideology. Identity explorations in adolescence involve trying out various possible future directions, especially in love and work, in the process of moving toward more stable choices that will provide the foundation for adult life.

This may have been true of adolescence when Erikson first proposed his theory in 1950, but much has changed since then. Because education lasts so long today, stable work is often not reached until about age thirty, and marriage and parenthood are entered for most people in the late twenties, the heart of identity explorations has moved from adolescence to emerging adulthood. Adolescents gain some experience with love, but they are more likely to be seeking a partner for next Saturday night than a partner for life. Only in emerging adulthood do explorations in love become identity based, as people seek a partner who will match them in ways that they hope will provide the foundation for a life-long relationship. Similarly, adolescents gain initial experience in work, but they tend to regard work as serving the function of providing money to enable them to lead an active leisure life. Only in emerging adulthood do explorations in work become more identity based, as people seek an occupation that matches their view of their abilities and interests, and that they hope will pay well enough to be promising as something they will devote themselves to for years to come.

What about the identity explorations of emerging adults who are aging out of care? Clearly, as the previous chapters describe, their opportunities for identity explorations in work are compromised by the time they reach emerging adulthood. Their rates of dropping out of secondary school are high. This severely limits their occupational options in emerging adulthood. Furthermore, they are unlikely to have the financial resources to obtain postsecondary education or training. Without family support to draw on and with only limited support from government programs, their focus in most cases must be on economic survival—on how to obtain a job that will allow them to make it from week to week without falling into poverty.

A variety of important questions remain that do not yet seem to have been addressed by research, on the basis of the previous chapters. Do emerging adults aging out of care have aspirations for higher education, even if the reality of obtaining it is elusive? What are their aspirations and goals in terms of the kind of job they will have as adults? What is the nature of their identity explorations with respect to love? Do they, like most other emerging adults, hope to find a "soulmate" who will be their ideal partner for life?[9] Or do they see their prospects for love as more limited, as they are in work?

The age of instability

Instability is a normative characteristic of emerging adulthood. The average number of job changes during the twenties in the United States is seven, meaning that the typical American emerging adult changes jobs nearly every year for a decade.[10] The twenties is also the decade when rates of residential changes are highest. During the mid-twenties, when the rate peaks, about 35 percent of emerging adults change residence every year.[11] This statistic reflects a wide variety of other aspects of instability, such as leaving home, returning home, leaving again, cohabiting, ending a cohabiting relationship, moving in with friends, and moving to a different area to pursue educational or occupational opportunities.

Although instability in emerging adulthood is the norm, it seems clear from the preceding chapters that the lives of emerging adults who are aging out of care are even more unstable than average. For example, in a study described by Tweddle in Chapter One, 90 percent of emerging adults who had been in care had moved in the past year, which makes the 35 percent normative figure seem modest. Emerging adults who had been in care are also at higher risk for aspects of instability such as homelessness and unemployment.

Clearly, emerging adulthood is the age of instability for persons aging out of care even more than for others.

Questions remain in this area as well. Are emerging adults aging out of care more unstable in love as well as in work and residence? That is, do they have more frequent changes of love partners? To what extent is the residential and work instability of emerging adults aging out of care a reflection of living on the edge of poverty, and to what extent is it for the same kinds of reasons as for other emerging adults, such as pursuing opportunities in education and work?

The self-focused age

Emerging adulthood is the self-focused age in the sense that it is the time of life that is the least subject to institutional control. Unlike children, adolescents, or adults, most emerging adults do not have family obligations that structure and circumscribe their lives. They are free to make their own decisions on a daily basis, from small decisions about what to eat for breakfast to larger decisions about how to spend their money and what job to pursue. Most emerging adults thrive on this freedom, as indicated in steadily rising rates of well-being during emerging adulthood and steadily declining rates of depressive affect.[12]

To what extent does this apply to emerging adults who have been in care? They are, in a sense, even less connected to institutional control than other emerging adults. Most emerging adults maintain some connection to their families of origin even after they have moved out, and they continue to receive some financial help from them through their early twenties.[13] In contrast, for emerging adults who have been in care, few of them have a regular connection to their family of origin by the time they reach their twenties.

Clearly, however, the lack of family connection and support experienced by emerging adults who have been in care does not bestow on them a freedom that allows them to be self-focused in their pursuit of self-development. On the contrary, their lack of family support is another aspect of their vulnerability. Most emerging adults voluntarily leave their family of origin when they reach emerging adulthood, in pursuit of greater freedom and independence.[14] For emerging adults who have been in care, their independence is forced on them when they reach the age when care is no longer provided by government institutions, formerly at age eighteen, now at age twenty-one in the United States and the United Kingdom. Being self-focused is something that is pursued as desirable for most emerging adults, in part because they know that if times get tough, they can always return home (as 40 percent do) or ask their parents to help them out financially.[15] For emerging adults who have been in care, their circumstances require them to be self-focused, whether they like it or not and whether they are ready or not.

Although it is possible to see emerging adulthood as the self-focused age for emerging adults in care, this has a different connotation for them than it does for other emerging adults. Still, it would be interesting to survey them and learn more about how they see it. Do they regard the point of aging out of care as beneficial in some ways? It means the end of government support for them, but it also means the end of government control over their lives. Once they age out of care, the government can no longer tell them where to live and with whom. Perhaps they see advantages in aging out of care, even as it also makes them more vulnerable in many ways.

The age of feeling in between

One of the most notable features of emerging adulthood is that it is a period in which most people feel as if they are neither adolescents nor adults but somewhere in between, on the way to adulthood but not there yet. In a variety of studies across various ethnic and socioeconomic groups within the United States and in studies of emerging adults in other industrialized countries as well, the majority of people who are aged eighteen to twenty-five respond to the question, "Do you feel that you have reached adulthood?" by answering neither yes nor no but, "In some ways yes, in some ways no."[16]

The ambiguity of emerging adults' self-perceptions with respect to their adult status is explained by the criteria they value most in marking the transition to adulthood. A surprising finding of this research is that the role transitions that have traditionally been assumed by researchers to define the transition to adulthood—finishing education, entering full-time work, marriage, and parenthood—have very little resonance with emerging adults as markers of their adult status. In fact, in the studies cited above, these role transitions consistently end up at the bottom of the list of criteria most favored as important in marking adulthood.

If the traditional criteria are no longer regarded by young people as important markers of adulthood, what is? Here too the picture is highly consistent across studies. The most important criteria virtually every time are accepting responsibility for one's actions, making independent decisions, and becoming financially independent. Each of these criteria is attained gradually, incrementally, which explains why emerging adults' sense of reaching adulthood is also gradual and incremental. Furthermore, each of the most important criteria is individualistic. In contrast to transitions such as marriage and parenthood, which constitute new and enduring obligations to others, the three top criteria are notable for how they symbolize the attainment of independence and self-sufficiency. Becoming an adult today means learning to stand alone as a self-sufficient person.

How does this feature apply to emerging adults aging out of care? It would seem likely that they do not have the luxury of proceeding gradually toward adulthood according to their own perceptions of when they are ready to accept responsibility for themselves, make independent decisions, and become financially independent. Rather, these things are thrust on them suddenly when they reach the age at which their government support runs out. Reaching that age means being required to stand alone and be self-sufficient, whether they feel ready for it or not. One would expect that they would be even less likely than other emerging adults to be ready for independence by age eighteen or even twenty-one, since they are less likely to have obtained the kinds of educational and occupational preparation that make a successful transition to independent living possible.

Still, here too it would be worth asking emerging adults aging out of care about their own views of their lives in these respects. Do they feel cheated out of the gradual, family-supported transition to adulthood that most of their peers have? Or did they already feel they had grown up faster than their peers due to the instability of their childhoods? Perhaps they even take pride in feeling ready to take on adult responsibilities and independent living before most of their peers do. It would certainly be interesting to ask them.

The age of possibilities

Emerging adulthood is the age of possibilities in two respects. First, it is the age of possibilities because it is the time of life when people have the greatest opportunity to change their lives in a potentially positive direction.[17] Children and adolescents are at the mercy of their parents. If their parents are reasonably well functioning, the children benefit, but if their parents have serious problems that affect family life, the children and adolescents suffer too. They cannot leave. If the parents' problems are so serious that they are unable to function with even minimal adequacy, the state takes over, but here too children and adolescents have little control. The state takes over the responsibilities normally held by the parents, but the children and adolescents have little voice in the matter.

Adults have more control over their lives than children or adolescents do, but adult life is usually structured by enduring commitments in love and work that are difficult to change once they are established. It is in emerging adulthood that people have the greatest opportunity for change. Free from the strictures of childhood and not yet committed to the role responsibilities of adulthood, emerging adults have the potential to change their lives in dramatic ways.

This has obvious relevance to aging out of care. The time of aging out of care is a period of great vulnerability, but for some emerging adults, it may be a time of great opportunity as well. Free at last from being controlled by either a dysfunctional family or a state bureaucracy, some of them may use their freedom to turn their lives in a new and better direction. How many? Under what circumstances? These are important questions to address.

The other way that emerging adulthood is the age of possibilities is that it tends to be a time of great expectations and high hopes for the future.[18] Even if their current lives are not going well—and this is often the case, as they change jobs and love partners frequently and struggle to find their place in the world—nearly all emerging adults believe that life will eventually be kind to them. They will find their soulmate, that person who is just right for them and who will love them forever. They will find that dream job that not only pays well but is enjoyable too—a form of self-expression, not just a way to put bread on the table. Nearly all of them believe that someday they will get to where they want to be in life.[19]

Do emerging adults aging out of care share this optimism or, due to their limited prospects, are they more pessimistic? This is a question worth asking. I can say that in my own research, I have found that limited prospects are no barrier to high hopes.[20] In fact, emerging adults from low socioeconomic status backgrounds are even more likely than emerging adults from high socioeconomic status backgrounds to believe their lives will be better than their parents' lives have been, perhaps because they start from a lower economic baseline. Emerging adults in care also start from a low baseline, since for most of them, their families were dysfunctional enough to have to have the state take over their care. Perhaps this generates optimism that they will have lives better than their parents' lives have been. Still, given the high rates of substance abuse and depression among emerging adults aging out of care, clearly not all of them are hopeful about their futures.

Conclusions and recommendations

The five features of emerging adulthood proposed as normative characteristics for emerging adults may apply to emerging adults aging out of care, but there is much that is unknown about how they see themselves and their lives. The features described here would be worth investigating further among emerging adults who have been in care, toward the goal of improving our understanding of their lives and needs.

It seems likely that most young people who age out of care experience emerging adulthood in some form. They may experience identity explorations, instability, a self-focused period, a sense of feeling in between adolescence and adulthood, and a sense of being at a time of life when the range of possibilities is unusually broad, even if the way they experience these things is different and in some ways more difficult than it is for other emerging adults.

Among the most important advice and assistance that could be given to young people aging out of care is to take contraceptive precautions if they are sexually active and do not intend to become pregnant. Having a child at an early age severely limits the potential of emerging adulthood as the age of possibilities, the time when a dramatic change for the better could be made. Pursuing educational options, occupational training, or a successful, independent way of life is difficult for emerging adults aging out of care, and adding the care of a young child to the tasks to be done stacks the odds even further against them.

Although the challenges facing emerging adults aging out of care are substantial, it is important to think of their emerging adult years in terms of not only their vulnerabilities but their potential strengths. Reaching the end of state support tosses them abruptly into the sometimes harsh realities of adult life, but for many of them, their saving grace may be that they are also at that time reaching a much greater potential for responsibility, skill development, and self-understanding than they had as adolescents. The challenge to policymakers and service providers is to think of creative ways to assist young people aging out of care in realizing emerging adulthood as the age of possibilities.

Notes

1. Hamilton, S., & Hamilton, M. A. (2006). School, work, and emerging adulthood. In J. J. Arnett & J. L. Tanner (Eds.), *Emerging adults in America: Coming of age in the 21st century* (pp. 257–277). Washington, DC: American Psychological Association.

2. Arnett, J. J. (2006a). Emerging adulthood: Understanding the new way of coming of age. In J. J. Arnett & J. L. Tanner (Eds.), *Emerging adults in America: Coming of age in the 21st century* (pp. 3–20). Washington, DC: American Psychological Association Press.

3. Arnett, J. J. (2004). *Emerging adulthood: The winding road from the late teens through the twenties.* New York: Oxford University Press.

4. Arnett, J. J. (2000). Emerging adulthood: A theory of development from the late teens through the twenties. *American Psychologist*, 55, 469–480; Arnett. (2004); Arnett & Tanner. (2006).

5. Arnett. (2004); Arnett, J. J. (2006b). The case for emerging adulthood in Europe. *Journal of Youth Studies*, 9, 111–123.

6. Reifman, A., Arnett, J. J., & Colwell, M. J. (2006). *The IDEA: Inventory of Dimensions of Emerging Adulthood.* Unpublished manuscript submitted for publication.

7. Arnett, J. J. (2005). The developmental context of substance use in emerging adulthood. *Journal of Drug Issues*, 35, 235–253.

8. Erikson, E. H. (1950). *Childhood and society.* New York: Norton.

9. Whitehead, B. D., & Popenoe, D. (2002). *Why wed? Young adults talk about sex, love, and first unions.* Report of the National Marriage Project, Rutgers, NJ. Retrieved August 4, 2003, from http://marriage.rutgers.edu/pubwhywe.htm.

10. U.S. Bureau of the Census. (2000). Statistical abstracts of the United States: 2000. Washington, DC: U.S. Bureau of the Census.

11. Arnett. (2004).

12. Galambos, N. L., Barker, E. T., & Krahn, H. J. (2006). Depression, anger, and self-esteem in emerging adulthood: Seven-year trajectories. *Developmental Psychology*, 4, 350–365.

13. Aquilino, W. S. (2006). Family relationships and support systems in emerging adulthood. In J. J. Arnett & J. Tanner (Eds.), *Coming of age in the 21st century: The lives and contexts of emerging adults* (pp. 193–218). Washington, DC: American Psychological Association.

14. Goldscheider, F., & Goldscheider, C. (1999). *The changing transition to adulthood: Leaving and returning home.* Thousand Oaks, CA: Sage.

15. Aquilino. (2006).

16. Arnett, J. (1994). Are college students adults? Their conceptions of the transition to adulthood. *Journal of Adult Development*, 1, 154–168; Arnett, J. J. (1997). Young people's conceptions of the transition to adulthood. *Youth and Society*, 29, 1–23; Arnett, J. J. (1998). Learning to stand alone: The contemporary American transition to adulthood in cultural and historical context. *Human Development*, 41, 295–315.

17. Masten, A. S., Obradovic, J., & Burt, K. B. (2006). Resilience in emerging adulthood: Developmental perspectives on continuity and transformation. In J. J. Arnett & J. L. Tanner (Eds.), *Emerging adults in America: Coming of age in the 21st century* (pp. 173–190). Washington, DC: American Psychological Association.

18. Arnett, J. J. (2000b). High hopes in a grim world: Emerging adults' views of their futures and of "Generation X." *Youth and Society*, 31, 267–286; Arnett. (2004).

19. Hornblower, M. (1997, June 9). Great Xpectations. *Time*, pp. 58–68.

20. Arnett. (2000b, 2004).

JEFFREY JENSEN ARNETT *is a research professor in the Department of Psychology at Clark University.*

Index

Abrams, L., 121
Administration of Families, 146
Adolescence: as age of feeling in between, 156–158; as age of possibilities, 158–159; identity challenge of, 153–154; instability characteristic of, 154–155; self-focus of, 155–156
Adoption and Children Act (2002) [UK], 44–45
Advancing Futures Bursary program (Alberta), 27
After Care Resource Centre (New South Wales), 46
Aftercare: Irish context of, 109; Loyola House program, 111–115; St. Xavier's Boys Home program for, 107–111; Scottish perspective on, 13, 119–136. *See also* Youth in transition
Alberta Youth in Transition initiative (2004), 27
Anglin, J., 130
Another Kind of Home report (Scotland), 124–125
Ansell-Casey Life Skills Assessments (ACLSA), 94–95, 100*fig*
Arnett, J. J., 8, 151, 161
Australia: After Care Resource Centre (New South Wales) of, 46; Special Youth Career Program (SYC) of, 45–46
Autonomous functioning: context and overview of the problem, 90–92; lessons learned from PQJ evaluation, 96–102; need for development of, 89–90; PQJ initiative to promote, 92–96

Baker, A.J.L., 91
Bell Canada Child Welfare Research Centre, 26

Bernstein, N., 78
Bobby, 60
Boy Scouts, 141
Boys Club of America, 141

California Youth Connection (CYC), 143–144
Canada: autonomous functioning of youth in care in, 89–102; future directions of service planning for youth in, 28–29; Health and Social Services Act of, 90; initiatives underway in, 26–28; MISWAA (Modernizing Income Security for Working Age Adults) of, 15; Youth Criminal Justice Act of, 90; Youth Protection Act of, 90; youth protection offered in Quebec, 12
Canada Learning Bond, 27–28
Canadian child welfare system: future directions of service planning by, 28–29; research on youth in transition from, 9–10; youth without citizenship leaving, 11–12, 77–88
Canadian Symposium on Child and Family Services Outcomes (2003), 26
CanLAC (Canadian version of Looking After Children), 26–27
Caplan, E., 85
Case management (Lighthouse ILP), 55
Casey Family Programs (U.S.), 40–41
Casey Foundation, 95
Casey, Jim, 40
Casey National Alumni Study (U.S.), 25–26
Catholic Children's Aid Society, 78
Cathy, 59–60
Cazabon, Andrée, 34
Centre of Excellence in Child Welfare (Canada), 34

163

Child Care Act (Section 45) [Ireland], 109
Child Welfare League of America (CWLA), 141, 146
Child Welfare League of Canada, 34, 79
Child Welfare Outcome Indicator Matrix (Canada), 26–27
Child Welfare Outcome Study (Canada), 26–27
Child welfare system: Australian, 45–46; Canadian, 9–12, 28–29, 77–78; changing to benefit youth, 65–67; examining youth expertise role in, 13; international studies on, 13, 18, 18–26, 107–115, 119–136; Scottish, 13, 119–136
Children at risk: in the developing world, 1; entering substitute care, 2–3; facilitating transition to independent living, 4–7; providing substitute care for, 1–2. *See also* Youth in care
Children (Leaving Care) Act [2000, UK], 18, 43–44
Children (Scotland) Act 1995 (CSA 1995), 125–126, 127, 131
Children's Act (1989) [UK], 42–43
Children's Aid Society (Canada), 11–12, 80
Children's Bureau, 146
Conseil permanent de la jeunesse (Quebec), 91
Corporate parenting concept, 127–131
Crisis management (Lighthouse ILP), 55
Crowe, K. M., 7, 13, 139, 149

"Day at the Capitol" (CYC annual event), 143
De-Witt-Wallace Foundation, 141
Dixon, J., 130, 132, 133

Education: as future success pillar, 36–37; poor outcomes for Scottish youth in care, 122
Emerging adulthood: as age of feeling in between, 156–158; as age of identity explorations, 153–154; as age of instability, 154–155; as age of possibilities, 158–159; definition of, 152; recommendations for facilitating, 159–160; as self-focused age, 155–156
Emotional healing, 39
Emotional support, 55
"Enrique's Journey" (*Los Angeles Times* series), 77–78
Erikson, E., 153

Financial support: debate over, 40; ILP program offering, 54
Former youth in care: Canadian research findings on, 16–17; emerging adulthood of, 152–160; international studies on outcomes of, 17–26. *See also* Youth in transition
Foster Care Alumni of America, 147
Foster Care Independence Act (FCIA) [U.S.], 25, 41–42, 140, 145
Foster care. *See* Substitute care (or alternative) living environment
Foster Club All Stars, 146–147
FosterClub, 146

Girl Club of America, 141
Girl Scouts, 141
Goffman, E., 129
Goyette, M., 7, 12, 89, 105
Groupe de recherche sur les inadaptations de l'enfance, 94

Hare, F. G., 7, 11, 77, 88
Health and Social Services Act (Canada), 90
Homelessness Act (2002) [UK], 44
Housing: cost considerations for, 72–73; developing independent living options for, 71–72; as future success pillar, 37–38; ILP program providing, 51–75; ILP's scattered-site apartment model for, 60–61; supervising youth in less restrictive, 62–65. *See also* Independent living

Identity: emerging adulthood as time for exploring, 153–154; as future success pillar, 38–39; Goffman's study on loss of, 129

INDEX   165

Independent living: definition and meaning of, 108; definitions of common options for, 53e; facilitating transition from care to, 4–7; Irish social care system aftercare approach to, 13, 108–115; Lighthouse Youth Services (ILP) program on, 51–75; preparing youth for, 69–75; supervising youth in, 62–65. *See also* Housing; Substitute care (or alternative) living environment; Youth in transition
Intergenerational interdependence norm, 34
International studies: on Australian child welfare programs, 45–46; characteristics of youth in, 18; on Irish child welfare system, 107–115; Scottish perspective on transition, 13, 119–136; U.S./UK findings on youth leaving care, 18–26
Ireland: examining the social care system of, 13; Loyola House program, 111–115; St. Xavier's Boys Home of, 107–111, 113, 114, 115; Section 45 (Child Care Act 1991) of, 109

John H. Chafee Foster Care Independence Program (U.S.), 25, 26, 140, 143

Kroner, M. J., 7, 11, 51, 75

Leaving Care: Throughcare and Aftercare in Scotland, 134
Life skills: as future success pillar, 38; ILP program offering training in, 55; preparing youth independent living, 71; promoting autonomous functioning, 89–102
"Life Skills Guidebook," 95
Lighthouse Youth Services (ILP) [U.S.]: assumptions underlying scattered-site apartment model used by, 60–62; case examples of youth in housing program, 58–60; examining outcomes of, 11; housing pilot program started by, 51–52; housing program description, 52, 54; lessons learning about supervising youth from, 62–63; lessons learning on transition process from, 67–75; measuring success of housing program, 56–58; risk management/liabiilty issues approach by, 63–65; transition services offered by, 54–56
Los Angeles Times, 77
Loyola House (Ireland), 111–115

McElwee, N., 7, 13, 107, 117
McKenna, S., 7, 13, 107, 117
Mann-Feder, V. R., 8
Martin, F., 16
Midwest Evaluation of Adult Functioning of Former Foster Youth: (U.S.), 25, 26
Millar, J., 7, 13, 117, 119, 137
Mincer, C., 91
MISWAA (Modernizing Income Security for Working Age Adults) [Toronto], 15
Multi-Site Evaluation of Foster Youth Programs (U.S.), 25, 26

National 4-H program, 141
National Collaboration for Youth, 141
National Foster Care Coalition, 140, 147
National Foster Care Month campaign, 140
National Independent Living Association, 140, 147
National Youth in Care Network (Canada), 34, 87
National Youth Development Bureau, 141
National Youth-in-Transition Database (U.S.), 25
Nazario, S., 77
Need to remourn, 6
New York Times, 77, 78

O'Connor, M., 7, 13, 107, 117
Olson, D., 91
The Orphan Country (Abrams), 121

Pape Adolescent Resource Centre (PRAC) [Toronto], 81–83

Pathways (assessment tool), 134–136
Poor Law (Scotland) Act 1845, 120
Portrait synthèse du jeune et de sa famille, 94
PQJ (Projet Qualification des jeunes) [Quebec]: assessment of youth in, 94–95, 97*t,* 100*fig;* clients served by, 93; description of program, 92-93; intervention objectives, process, and strategies, 94–96
Promoting Positive Outcomes for Youth From Care Project (University of Victoria), 17

Quarriers Homes (England), 121

Regina, 56–57
Reid, C., 7, 10, 33, 49
Relationships: adolescence explorations with, 153; as future success pillar, 36; PQJ evaluation lessons on issues of, 96-99
Remourning, 6

St. Xavier's Boys Home (Ireland): comparing Loyola House to, 113, 114; description and focus of, 107–108; key worker system at, 110–111; lessons learned from, 115; milestones used at, 111; supportive and consistent environment of, 109–110
SARIMM (Service d'aide aux réfugiés et aux immigrants du Montréal Métropolitain) [Quebec], 85–86, 87
Scattered-site apartment program model (Lighthouse ILP), 60–61
Scottish child welfare system: *Another Kind of Home* report on, 124–125; aspiration and inspirations for, 126–127; challenge of aftercare of young offenders in, 123–124; Children (Scottish child welfare system) Act 1995 (CSA 1995), 125–126, 127, 131; corporate parenting concept used in, 127-131; examining care/aftercare practices by, 13, 119; needs not deeds approach by, 122–123; Pathways assessment tool, 134–136; poor educational/economic outcomes of youth in,

122; Poor Law (Scotland) Act 1845, 120; Social Work (Scotland) Act 1968, 122; *Still a Bairn?* report, 132–134; Supporting Young People in Scotland: and, 133–134; Victorian cultural/historic factors impacting, 120–122, 126
Section 45 (Child Care Act 1991) [Ireland], 109
Separated child, 78–79
September 11, 2001, 78
Silva-Wayne, S., 16
Social Work (Scotland) Act 1968, 122
Solidarité Jeunesse program (Quebec), 90
Special Youth Career Program (SYC) [Australia], 45–46
Standards of Excellence for Transition, Independent Living and Self-Sufficiency Services (TILSS), 141
Stein, M., 130, 132, 133
Still a Bairn? report (Scotland), 132–134
Substitute care (or alternative) living environment: Casey Family Programs (U.S.) as private, 40–41; challenges of, 3–4; definition of term, 90; entering, 2–3; facilitating transition to independent living, 4–7; leaving, 4–6; providing children at risk with, 1–2. *See also* Independent living; Youth in care
Supporting Young People in Scotland:, 133

TILSS (Transition, Independent Living and Self-Sufficiency Services), 141
Title IV-E Independent Living Initiative (1986) [U.S.], 25
Toronto Globe and Mail, 77
Transition from care. *See* Youth in transition
Transitional Year Program (University of Toronto), 27
Trevor, 59
Tweddle, A., 7, 9, 15, 31

UN Convention on the Rights of the Child, 80, 87–88
Unaccompanied minors: future directions of studies/policies for, 87–88;

interviews with child welfare personnel on, 81–83; interviews with others regarding, 85–86; interviews with, 83–85; literature on, 78–80; preliminary implications regarding, 86–87; study of Canadian welfare system and, 11–12, 77–88; transition and vulnerability of, 80–81
UNHCR (United Nations High Commission for Refugees), 79, 80
United Kingdom: Adoption and Children Act (2002) of, 44–45; Children (Leaving Care) Act [2000] of, 18, 43–44; Children's Act (1989) of, 42–43; Homelessness Act (2002) of, 44; youth leaving care studies in, 18–25
United Nations High Commission for Refugees (UNHCR), 79, 80
United States: Casey Family Programs of, 40–41; Foster Care Independence Act (FCIA) of, 25, 41–42, 140, 145; Title IV-E Independent Living Initiative (1986) of, 25; youth leaving care studies in, 18–25
University of Toronto's Transitional Year Program, 27
University of Victoria (Canada), 17
University of York (Scotland), 132
U.S. Department of Health, Education and Welfare, 140–141
U.S. Department of Health and Human Services, 25, 146
U.S. Homeland Security, 78
U.S. Homeland Security Immigration Statistics Yearbook, 79
U.S. Immigration and Naturalization Service, 78

Voices for America's Children (U.S.), 25

Wards of the Crown (film), 34

YMCA, 141
Youth advisory boards, 142–145
Youth in care: increasing number of, 16; MISWAA study of, 15; promoting autonomous functioning of, 89–102.
See also Children at risk; Former youth in care; Substitute care (or alternative) living environment
Youth Criminal Justice Act (Canada), 90
Youth development: incorporating youth expertise partnership in, 142–148; programs for, 140–142
Youth engagement: as future success pillar, 39; through involvement in service planning, 142–148
Youth expertise: embracing youth as partners through, 139; examining use of, 13; including at macro level of planning, 146–147; including at micro level of service design, 145–146; interviews with unaccompanied minors, 83–85; moving beyond youth advisory boards, 142–145; recommendations for successful transition by Canadian, 28-29
Youth Protection Act (Canada), 90
Youth in transition: Canadian research on, 9–10; Casey study predicting outcomes for, 25–26; examining international examples of best practices, 10–11; facilitating process of, 4–7; future directions of Canadian service planning for, 28–29; international studies on, 18–26; Irish social care system approach to, 13, 107–115; lessons learned about, 67–75; need to remourn and, 6; research on process of, 33–34; seven pillars and foundation for, 35–40; study of unaccompanied minors in Canada, 11–12, 77–88; supervising in less restrictive housing, 62–65. *See also* Aftercare; Former youth in care; Independent living
Youth in Transition initiative (2004) [Alberta], 27
Youth in transition pillars: education, 36–37; emotional healing, 39; foundation of financial support, 40; housing, 37–38; identity, 38–39; life skills, 38; relationships, 36; youth engagement, 39

NEW DIRECTIONS FOR YOUTH DEVELOPMENT
Order Form
SUBSCRIPTIONS AND SINGLE ISSUES

DISCOUNTED BACK ISSUES:

Use this form to receive **20% off** all back issues of New Directions for Youth Development. All single issues priced at **$23.20** (normally $29.00)

TITLE	ISSUE NO.	ISBN

Call 888-378-2537 or see mailing instructions below. When calling, mention the promotional code, **JB7ND**, to receive your discount.

SUBSCRIPTIONS: *(1 year, 4 issues)*

☐ New Order ☐ Renewal

U.S.	☐ Individual: $80	☐ Institutional: $195
Canada/Mexico	☐ Individual: $80	☐ Institutional: $235
All Others	☐ Individual: $104	☐ Institutional: $269

Call 888-378-2537 or see mailing and pricing instructions below. Online subscriptions are available at www.interscience.wiley.com.

Copy or detach page and send to:
**John Wiley & Sons, Journals Dept, 5th Floor
989 Market Street, San Francisco, CA 94103-1741**
Order Form can also be faxed to: 888-481-2665

Issue/Subscription Amount: $ _____
Shipping Amount: $ _____
(for single issues only—subscription prices include shipping)
Total Amount: $ _____

SHIPPING CHARGES:
SURFAC   Domestic   Canadian
First Item $5.00 $6.00
Each Add'l Item $3.00 $1.50

(No sales tax for U.S. subscriptions. Canadian residents, add GST for subscription orders. Individual rate subscriptions must be paid by personal check or credit card. Individual rate subscriptions may not be resold as library copies.)

☐ Payment enclosed (U.S. check or money order only. All payments must be in U.S. dollars.)
☐ VISA ☐ MC ☐ Amex # _____ Exp. Date _____
Card Holder Name _____ Card Issue # _____
Signature _____ Day Phone _____
☐ Bill Me (U.S. institutional orders only. Purchase order required.)
Purchase order # _____
                    Federal Tax ID13559302   GST 89102 8052
Name _____
Address _____
Phone _____ E-mail _____

JB7ND

NEW DIRECTIONS FOR YOUTH DEVELOPMENT IS NOW AVAILABLE ONLINE AT WILEY INTERSCIENCE

What is Wiley InterScience?

Wiley InterScience is the dynamic online content service from John Wiley & Sons delivering the full text of over 300 leading scientific, technical, medical, and professional journals, plus major reference works, the acclaimed *Current Protocols* laboratory manuals, and even the full text of select Wiley print books online.

What are some special features of Wiley InterScience?

Wiley InterScience Alerts is a service that delivers table of contents via e-mail for any journal available on Wiley InterScience as soon as a new issue is published online.

Early View is Wiley's exclusive service presenting individual articles online as soon as they are ready, even before the release of the compiled print issue. These articles are complete, peer-reviewed, and citable.

CrossRef is the innovative multi-publisher reference linking system enabling readers to move seamlessly from a reference in a journal article to the cited publication, typically located on a different server and published by a different publisher.

362.7083 T772   INFCW
Transition or eviction : youth exiting care for independent living /

CENTRAL LIBRARY
11/10

Friends of the
Houston Public Library

Guest Users can browse Wiley InterScience for unrestricted access to journal Tables of Contents and Article Abstracts, or use the powerful search engine.
Registered Users are provided with a *Personal Home Page* to store and manage customized alerts, searches, and links to favorite journals and articles. Additionally, Registered Users can view free Online Sample Issues and preview selected material from major reference works.
Licensed Customers are entitled to access full-text journal articles in PDF, with select journals also offering full-text HTML.

How do I become an Authorized User?

Authorized Users are individuals authorized by a paying Customer to have access to the journals in Wiley InterScience. For example, a university that subscribes to Wiley journals is considered to be the Customer. Faculty, staff, and students authorized by the university to have access to those journals in Wiley InterScience are Authorized Users. Users should contact their Library for information on which Wiley journals they have access to in Wiley InterScience.

ASK YOUR INSTITUTION ABOUT WILEY INTERSCIENCE TODAY!